Un

Marx

Friedrich W. Sixel

University Press of America, Inc.
Lanham • New York • London

4720 Boston Way
Lanham, Maryland 20706

3 Henrietta Street
London, WC2E 8LU England

Printed in the United States of America
British Cataloging in Publication Information Available

Library of Congress Cataloging-in-Publication Data

Sixel, Friedrich W.
Understanding Marx/ Friedrich W. Sixel
p. cm.
Includes bibliographical references.
1. Marx, Karl, 1818-1883. Grundrisse der Kritik der politischen Ökonomie. 2. Marxian economics. 3. Philosophy, Marxist.
4. Dialectical materialism. I. Title.
HB97.5.S5378 1995 335.4'12--dc20 95-24031 CIP

ISBN 0–7618–0024–7 (cloth: alk. paper)
ISBN 0–7618–0025–5 (pbk.: alk. paper)

™The paper used in this publication meets the minimum requirements of American National Standard for Information Sciences—Permanence of Paper for Printed Library Materials, ANSI Z39.48–1984.

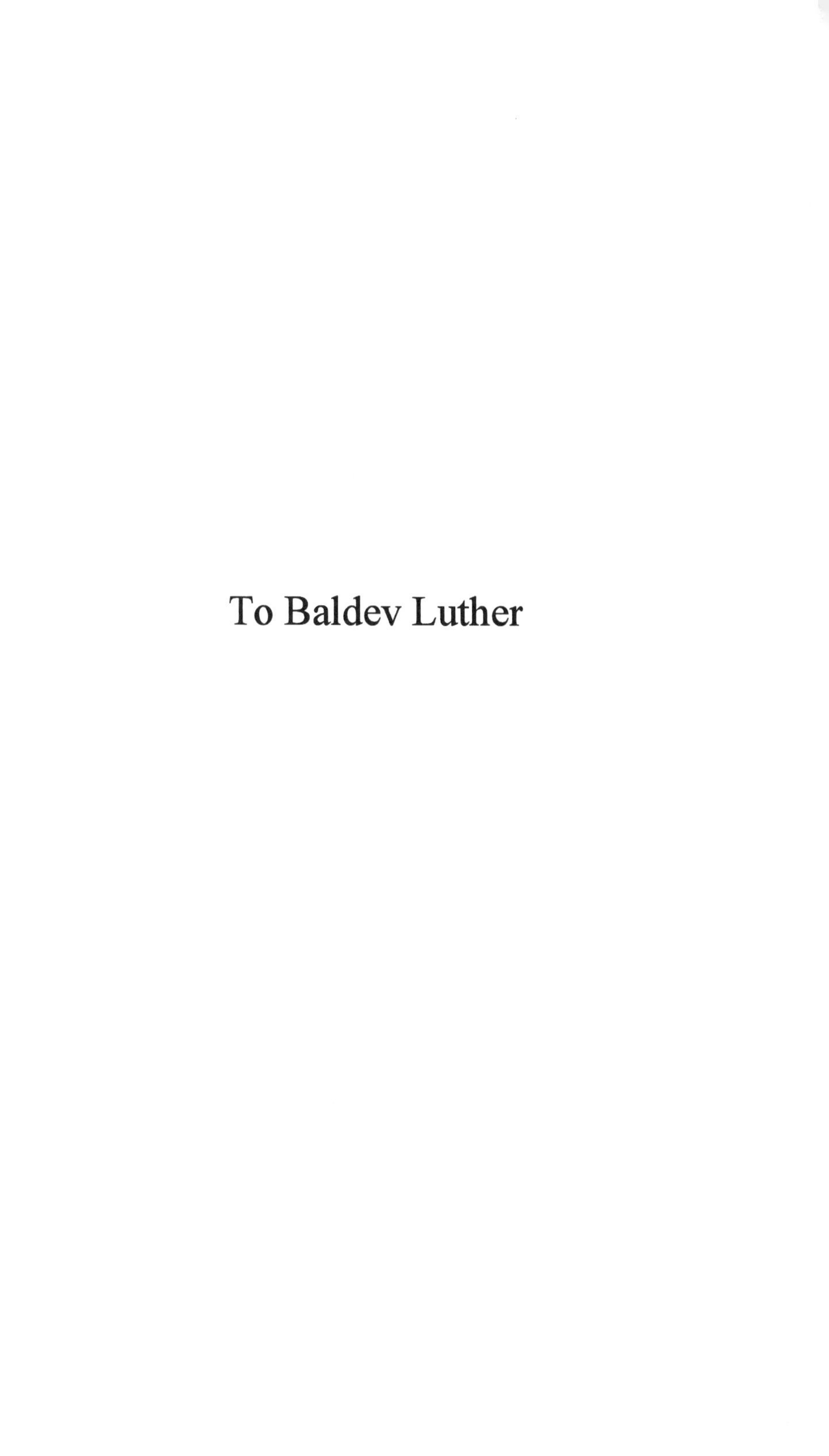

To Baldev Luther

Contents

Preface

I know Marx is not "in". But since quite some time I have been unhappy that his distortion was, both in the West and in the East. In the East, Marx was compulsory reading, while much of his work was off limits, at least for the wider public. In the West, all of his publications were readily available for study, and yet many of "the Marxists" I met had hardly ever read more than a few passages of what he wrote. When I discovered Marx, together with some friends in the early 60s, we immediately sensed that something of extraordinary dimensions was before us, and, as studies progressed, we came to know how much it would take to fathom the depth of his thought.

In the early 1970s, a few years after coming to Queen's University in Canada, I was asked to teach a course in the Sociology of Economic Development. Ever since, with the exception of a year or two, I have taught this course enjoying the enrolment of Undergraduate and Graduate Students in it coming from such diverse fields as Sociology, Economics, History, Philosophy, Political Studies and Geography.

It was no question for me that Marx had to be a departure point for dealing with contemporary problems in Development. At the same time, the often stated suggestion that I was "applying" Marx in that course left me baffled. Quite a few students who took that course came to understand that such an application was not intended and that, in fact, it was antagonistic to Marx's thinking. This insight of theirs was quite supportive and rewarding for me, and therefore I would like to thank them for having been partners in dialogue for me in all those years in which I taught Socy 472/872.

It is, of course, one thing to know that one wishes to introduce people to Marx's style of thinking, and it is quite another to practically do that. Not even one volume of the major editions of his works could be expected to be read in a one-semester course. So, I decided in the fall of 1972, when launching the course, to have students read the "Introduction" to the "*Grundrisse*" (and selected passages from its main body), taking advantage of the circumstance that this piece would (finally) appear in English shortly after; in fact, it came out in 1973. Ever since, the "Introduction" and selected passages from the "*Grundrisse*" have remained central to my course.

Quite a few students and friends have urged me to publish my interpretation of Marx as based on the sections from the "*Grundrisse*" selected for my class. For quite some time I was reluctant to do that, because I knew that writing commentaries even on only the central points that Marx made in the "*Grundrisse*" would explode into several hundred if not over thousand of pages to be filled with ink.

The one person, however, who was most persistent in his urging to publish "at least your commentary on the 'Introduction'" was my friend and comrade Baldev Luther. Through many, many discussions stretching over more than twenty years and ranging from Marx to Bloch, from Indian history to Goethe's Teachings on Color, he had a constant influence on my thought. I finally gave in to his idea to pen down my interpretation of that "Introduction". Virtually every line of my commentary on it, as it follows here, has been discussed with him so that it is only a small expression of my gratitude that I dedicate my "Understanding Marx" to him.

Needless to say though, it would be problematic to ground one's understanding of Marx on just one short piece of his gigantic oeuvre, however suitable that particular piece may be. It is for this reason, among others, that I have included a good many references here to other parts of his writings, although I have limited them to those that came readily to mind (ignoring the occasional authorship of Friedrich Engels). In other words, completeness in this regard is not intended. And yet, these references may still serve the purpose of giving the reader an incentive to further explore the richness and dynamics of Marx's thought, as it has suffered so often from narrow-minded, dogmatic and impoverished interpretation.

I would also like to extend my special thanks to the secretarial staff at the Queen's Sociology Department, particularly to Geetha Rengan, Carolyn Hider and June Pilfold. They used every moment in which administrative matters were not on their hands to type out my manuscript. They even corrected it on quite a few occasions where my eyes had overlooked mistakes. While this was already a gratifying sign of interest in my work, their request for a copy of my commentary made me very happy indeed. So, to the three of them: thanks a lot and stay alive as you are!

Finally, I would like to mention the help of Shirley Fraser from the Department of Political Studies at Queen's. She formatted and printed the final version of the whole book. As always, she did a marvellous job. And, of course, I should not forget who helped me proofread the text in all its detail: Carlos Neves, a Graduate Student at our Department and, beyond that, a good friend of mine. I would like to thank both, Shirley and Carlos, very much.

Last but not least, I wish to point out that numerous quotations have been taken, for use in the present text, from the "Introduction" (pp. 83-111) to the "*Grundrisse*" by Karl Marx, translated by Martin Nicolaus (Penguin Books 1973, in association with New Left Review), translation copyright © Martin Nicolaus 1973. These quotations have been reproduced by written permission of Penguin Books Ltd.; for the granting of this permission I wish to express my sincere thanks.

Introduction: Aspects in the Study of Marx

Over the years, I have come to see that an adequate understanding of Marx has to overcome three kinds of difficulties. These are, presented in the sequence of their growing complexity, the following ones:

1. Marx uses a good many concepts without ever defining them and he uses them in ways quite often different from how most people understand them today. As being among these concepts, I would like to mention production, totality, generality, mediation, identity, abstraction, spontaneity, and critique, for example. The reason that Marx does hardly ever define these concepts lies with the circumstance that they were used widely in their particular way among philosophers in his day and age. This gives us a good reason to understand Marx from within the context of the tradition in which he stands.

2. This tradition is definitely not that of analytical thought. On the contrary, his thinking is deeply permeated by the awareness that all human judgements are synthetic in nature, i.e. involve the subjectivity of those who make them[1]. Therefore, reading Marx in

[1]It should be noted that, until quite recently, it was thought that there were at least a few kinds of statements possible in which the predicate was contained in the grammatical subject or, to put it differently, it was thought that statements would be possible that would hold without being dependent

terms of what is today's dominant mode of thinking, namely the analytical one, means misreading him fundamentally. Even an awareness of the neo-positivist notion of the contingent nature of judgements would do little for an effort to understand him. Particularly, Marx's conceptualization of the dynamic nature of the human subject and thus of the dynamic nature of truth will be negatively affected by a reading carried out in terms of the epistemological opportunism that prevails in contemporary thought.

3. Certainly, Marx's sense for the relativity of truth and thus the historicity of the human subject seems to backfire at his own so-called position, shall we say that of Dialectical Materialism[2]. But it does do that only in appearance and only for those who misunderstand Dialectical Materialism. Marx's own relativization of his own thought - we have to come back to this - is in fact a confirmation for the merely temporary validity of ideas. The primacy of matter, not the concept of the primacy of matter, reasserts itself in

---

on the human subject who makes these statements. If existent, such statements could be thought of as analytical ones. An example for such a statement would be a tautology or a definition like "a ball is round". Even this view has been abandoned today within the synthetic tradition. Now all statements are seen as synthetic, i.e. are seen as holding, because they imply the nature of the speaker. For another kind of subject, e.g. for God, human statements would not hold. See also pp.4f. For Marx's philosophical concern, i.e. for his study of Political Economy, the involvement of the human subject, both in speech and act, i.e. in theory and praxis, is obviously beyond question. For him, analytical statements are, as unthinkable as productive activities would be without a human subject.

[2]I would like to point out that Marx uses the term Dialectical Materialism (or Historical Materialism for that matter) very rarely. The only occasion I have seen him do that was in an article titled "*Quid pro Quo*", published in "*Das Volk*", edition of 6 Aug. 1859; see *Marx-Engels-Werke* (widely known as MEW and referred to as such throughout this essay), XIII, 454ff. This circumstance does, however, not keep me from using this label for his philosophy. I do so, because it allows me to indicate that Marx's thought is materially grounded and is aware of the material relation between our species and the world of matter around it.

a style of thinking that does not take thought, mental constructs or strategically placed paradigms as its departure point, but takes off from the materialness in which it itself occurs. It may not be too much to claim for Marx that he knew the material essence of thinking itself. The claim that nature could return to itself in the *nature* of man's thinking is a consideration that would, without a question, be in line with his thinking[3].

I shall now try to unfold Marx's thought not in the sequence of these three aspects but in view of them. This will be done as promised, by first contextualizing Marx philosophically[4]. Later on, and in much greater detail, I will present an interpretive commentary on Marx's "Introduction" to the "*Grundrisse*", a draft of "The

---

[3]Consider, e.g., the following passages: MEW, III, 30; EB (*Ergänzungsband*, i.e. Supplementary Volume, always quoted here by using the traditional abbreviation EB) I, 536, 543f, 586.

[4]My rather brief contextualization of Marx's thought will not be accompanied by footnotes from the secondary literature. However, I would like to identify a few of those numerous publications that have shaped my understanding of his background:

Adler, Max: *Das Soziologische in Kant's Erkenntniskritik*, Vienna (*Verlag der Wiener Volksbuchhandlung*) 1924.

Barion, Jakob: *Hegel und die marxistische Staatslehre*, Bonn (*Bouvier Verlag*) 1970.

Bloch, Ernst: *Das Prinzip Hoffnung*, Frankfurt (*Suhrkamp Verlag*) 1959.

Habermas, Jürgen: *Erkenntnis und Interesse*, Frankfurt (*Suhrkamp Verlag*) 1968 (particularly Part 1).

Martin, Gottfried: *Immanuel Kant - Ontologie und Wissenschaftstheorie*, Cologne (*Kölner Universitätsverlag*) 1958.

Schmied-Kowarzik, Wolfdietrich: *Das dialektische Verhältnis des Menschen zur Natur*, Freiburg, Munich (*Verlag Karl Alber*) 1984.

Schmidt, Alfred: *Der Begriff der Natur in der Lehre von Marx*, Frankfurt (*Europäische Verlagsanstalt*) 1962.

Capital" written in fall and winter of 1857/58[5]. I want to focus on

---

[5]The "Introduction" was actually written in Aug./Sept. 1857, i.e. prior to Marx's work on the text of the "*Grundrisse*" itself. Both manuscripts were put on paper by Marx in the rather provisional form of a rough draft never meant to be published. Foreign Language Publishers (Moscow) published the "Introduction", the "*Grundrisse*" and some miscellaneous texts written by Marx between 1850 and 1859 together in two volumes in 1939 and 1941 respectively. The publication of these two volumes was based on the editiorial work done by the Marx-Engels-Lenin Institute (Moscow). Very few copies of this Moscow edition have made their way into the West.
In 1953, the *Dietz Verlag*, (East-) Berlin, produced a photo offset reprint of the two volumes of the Moscow edition, but published them in one. This publication has omitted a few illustrations and facsimiles contained in the Moscow edition; the text, however, was left untouched. This offset reprint was edited again by the *Dietz Verlag* in 1974.
An undated photo reproduction of the Moscow edition, also put into one volume and shortened by omitting illustrations and facsimiles as well, but omitting nothing of the text, was published by the *Europäische Verlagsanstalt* (Frankfurt) and the *Europa Verlag* (Vienna) later, probably during the 1960s.
My commentary on the "Introduction" is based on the English translation of the "Introduction" (and the "*Grundrisse*") as made by Martin Nicolaus and published in 1973 by Penguin Books in association with New Left Review. The translator has used the version published by the *Dietz Verlag*, (East-) Berlin in 1953.
In addition, Nicolaus' translation is informed by a more recent German edition of the "Introduction" published by the *Dietz Verlag*, (East-) Berlin. This edition of the "Introduction" and the "*Grundrisse*" is based on a new study of Marx's manuscript. The result of this study seems to differ from the older editions (which go back to the 1939/41 edition) only with regard to "minor particulars", as Nicolaus puts it.
Since both the undated publication and the 1953 publication by the *Dietz Verlag* are photo reproductions of one and the same edition, namely the Moscow edition, and since the Nicolaus translation is influenced by the most recent German edition only with regard to "minor particulars", I felt it justified to use the undated edition as a reference for checking on the Nicolaus translation of the "Introduction". Of course, should the Nicolaus translation differ from the undated German version with regard to those

that piece, because Marx discusses matters there in a cohesiveness which has rarely found repetition in other parts of his work[6].

---

minor particulars in the passages selected for my commentary, I will take note of these differences.

With regard to these bibliographical remarks, see Marx, 1973 "Foreword", (especially footnote 1) and the "Note of the Translator" added there. See also Marx, n.d., "*Zur vorliegenden Ausgabe*".

The secondary literature so often makes the claim that much of Marx's writings prior to "The Capital" was unknown to his followers until the 20s and 30s of this century when these writings were first published. This, however, is not the case as far as the "Introduction" to the "*Grundrisse*" is concerned. Karl Kautsky, the former personal secretary of Friedrich Engels and later theoretician of the Party, published the "Introduction" in the journal "*Die Neue Zeit*" in 1903 and again in his "*Zur Kritik der politischen Ökonomie*" in 1907. It should be noted, though, that Kautsky created a heavily edited version of the "Introduction", obviously with the intent of making this important piece accessible to a wider audience. Hans-Joachim Lieber and Benedikt Kautsky have published Karl Kautsky's version of the "Introduction" in vol. VI, 793-833 of their "*Karl Marx Ausgabe*", Darmstadt (*Wiss. Buchgesellschaft*) 1964 (republished ibid. 1971).

[6]The reader may want to know Marx's reason for not including this "Introduction" into what later became the final version of the "*Grundrisse*", namely "*Das Kapital*". He had already omitted this "Introduction" in "*Zur Kritik der Politischen Ökonomie*" (see MEW, XIII) where he makes the following remark on the "Introduction" in the second paragraph of the Preface to "*Zur Kritik...*". We read: "I suppress a general Introduction which I had penned down, because, on second thought, every anticipation of results yet to be proven appeared to be distracting and because the reader who wishes to follow me should be willing to rise from the particular to the general" (my translation, FWS) and not the other way around, one might add.

Part I

Marx's Philosophical Background - A Contextualization

It is well known that Friedrich Engels thought that the great accomplishments of German Philosophy since Immanuel Kant had found their culmination in Marx's Dialectical Materialism[7]. We speak of this tradition as the critical tradition, simply because its members are most of the time engaged in what they call "critiques". Kant wrote, for instance, his three critiques; Hegel's philosophy originates in his critique of Kant; Marx critiques Hegel and ends up writing a "Critique of Political Economy"[8]; and today's "Critical Sociology" claims to perpetuate that tradition by attempting a critique of today's ideology. Critique in that tradition involves, first of all, the attempt

---

[7]See M E G A , (i.e. *Marx-Engels-Gesamtausgabe*, usually abbreviated as MEGA) I, 446, 448.

[8]Marx's objection against a merely philosophical critique is, of course, elaborated upon in his "The Holy Family", MEW, II, 3-223, in his "Theses on Feuerbach", MEW, III 5-7, and in his "The German Ideology" MEW, III, 9-530. It is perhaps interesting to note, in this connection, that he sees Feuerbach and not so much himself as *the* critic of Hegel's Philosophy, see MEW, II, 147.

to understand a thought system (philosophy, culture, theory, etc.) on its own terms. Questions are asked which aim at understanding the totality of such a thought system including the ultimate premises, axioms and a-priori concepts on which it rests. Of course, the questions raised may lead to embarrassment of the thought inspected because positions held by it, may turn out to be untenable, because they are contradictory in themselves, i.e. on their own terms.

In this event, an attempt of understanding owes it to itself to identify precisely the point of contradiction within the thought system concerned. This is to say that at that point understanding changes into critique. To the extent that that change can occur at any time in the course of asking questions, we see that understanding is contained in and comes out of an awareness of a possible failure in explanations given. This is to say then that the innocence and good intentions of understanding spill over into the critique.

This containment implies a peculiar dimension of critique. It needs to be emphasized, in this connection, that a critique sets in and is based on the friendly acceptance of concepts immanent in the thought inspected. And yet, if it is not able to accept the assumptions proposed and the conclusions drawn, then the asking of questions turns into a critique. There is one thing a critique is certainly not: it is not an imposition of notions foreign to the ideas to be understood. Such an imposition would pervert critique into a mere criticism. This is to say then that even the determinate negation of internal contradictions includes an invitation to change the thought system under inspection jointly, i.e. in an agreement between those critiqued and the others doing the critiquing. Of course, attempts at understanding will not always end up in problems. They may very well succeed and then unveil the true and tenable premises of a thought structure. And yet, in such cases an attempt of understanding is still called in that tradition a critique, probably out of the awareness that understanding may change into a critique in the narrower sense at any moment in the process of understanding.

Kant's "Critique of Pure Reason" provides us with an example of successful understanding. As such, it allows us to elaborate a bit further on the concepts of critique and contradiction and to connect them with the rather complex concept of totality.

It was Kant's intent to fully understand Newton's mechanics with regard to both the totality of its range and the conceptual conditions for its possibility. This is to say Kant tried to mentally connect the entirety of Newton's findings on mechanics without leaving aside a single one of them. The making of all mental connections implies the absence of contradictions, while, turning this statement around, the detection of a contradiction would shatter the coherence and thus the mental acceptability of the thought. This is to say that sense can only be where it is totally understood sense.

In addition, the critical tradition also knows that true understanding is only accomplished when the ultimate premises of a body of thought can be shared by, shall we say, writer and reader. Only then is a body of thought conceptually accounted for. Kant believed that he had discovered the twelve concepts that underlie Newton's mechanics, i.e. that he had managed to reduce the complexity of Newton's mechanics to twelve underlying concepts. These twelve concepts were no longer reducible to any other more fundamental concepts. He speaks of these twelve concepts as categories or a-priori concepts. He understood them as having logical primacy over Newton's empirical findings. As ultimate terms of reference, they made Newton's investigations possible, i.e. they were the conditions for his theory on mechanics.

In other words, the totality of Newton's mechanics could be constructed out of the twelve categories without any contradiction. But they are not only a consistent part of Newton's knowledge of the mechanical world, i.e. fit into that knowledge without contradiction, they also contain the totality of it, so that we come across here the somewhat surprising claim that a totality is contained in what is only one of its parts. Later, Marx has no difficulty with such a notion; it is a constitutive aspect of his thinking.

To the extent that Kant saw in Newton's mechanics the purest kind of knowledge ever possible, he understood his table of twelve categories (composed of multitude, totality, reality, negation, limitation, inherentness, causality, correlation, possibility, being [*Dasein*], necessity) as being fundamental for all knowledge. As such, these categories, according to Kant, also provide us with the ultimate condition for the possibility of the being of all those things of which we could have knowledge at all. In other words, the twelve categories do not mediate the world of objects to us simply because they are the properties of the mind; they are also properties of the objects as we know them. The twelve categories do not mediate the world to us by way of being our instruments, they mediate our thinking with the world, because they underlie the possibility of the world of objects to be and the possibility for our thinking to gain knowledge of that world of objects. In Kantian words: the identity between the world and our knowledge rests on the identity between our categories and the logical structure of the world. Because of the mediating nature of these categories, they comprise the totality of all that has being for us and is thinkable for us.

The notion of "for us" is introduced here not so much because it allowed Kant to point out that we can never know what things are for themselves and in themselves, but because this notion leads us to understand what Kant and the whole critical tradition understood by the concept of synthesis. We need to understand that concept, because it is essential for our understanding of Hegel's and Marx's dialectics as well.

It is well known that Kant distinguished between analytical and synthetic statements. If we say, e.g. that the sum total of the three angles in a triangle drawn in one plane equals 180°, then we have to keep silently in mind that this statement holds only for us as human subjects; we synthesize, so to speak, our own subjectivity, here with regard to our ways of viewing, into that statement; it holds *for us*. Would our ways of viewing be different, our statements about what we see would have to be different too. Today the critical tradition is aware of the circumstance that all statements are synthetic in nature; they do not hold for objects in themselves as the analytical tradition maintains, but only for objects as they have a being for our kind of subjectivity.

The subjectivity constitutive for the making of synthetic statements requires, for Kant, yet another aspect. Categories cannot, by themselves, fully account for their coming to work. Kant identifies a driving force "behind" the twelve categories which pushes them to reach out into the world of objects. He calls this force "spontaneity". Judgements are, therefore, not only synthetic products of the mind, i.e. of the twelve categories, but also of man's, at least initially, unreflected will-power. This will-power is unreflected, i.e. spontaneous, because it lies equally with the categories at an a-priori level; it has to be postulated as logically preceding any act of thinking.

Kant's philosophy thus contains, within the concept of spontaneity, a dimension which is of a surprisingly non-mentalistic nature. In addition, we have to note that it constitutes a second leg for his theory of cognition without which that theory could not stand. Given the sameness in level of significance, it is quite surprising that Kant fails to devote equal attention to spontaneity as to that given to the categories. Could it not be that an exploration of spontaneity would have allowed him to uncover a possibly material, i.e. nature-given, foundation of thinking? Instead, Kant's interest focusses on mental a-prioris and their commonality with the world out there, that is to say with the world not in its material-ness, but in its logical structure.

Certainly, Kant was aware that judgements are at any rate mental abstractions about objects and not concrete things themselves at least as far as their meaning goes. He demanded of judgements that they lend themselves to be "schematized" in this concrete world; only such abstractions were admissible for him. Abstractions that could not be grounded in some concrete objects were considered as "empty" abstractions and therefore rejected.

This way Kant secures his concept of identity between the subject and the world of objects, but he does so at the cost of reducing the human subject to what is practically only a categorical mind-set. At the same time, his demand that abstractions must not be empty remains unfounded. At this point, the question arises again and from a slightly different angle, whether a deeper exploration of spontaneity would not only have enriched, but also challenged his Idealism.

And yet, Kant's philosophy was understood by Friedrich Engels as a statement on man's "communist essence". This may come to most of us as a surprise. Nonetheless we have to appreciate that Kant understood the twelve categories as properties of all human beings. He saw them as describing the human commonality; they constituted our species-being. This is to say that our subjectivity does not only tie us into the world out there qua the categorical make-up which we share with it, this subjectivity also mediates each one of us with all of us. This is what allowed Engels to speak of man's "communist essence", and this same circumstance is also at the root of Marx's concept of the double dialectic between nature and man, on the one hand, and man and society, on the other[9].

While concepts like man's "communist essence" or "double dialectic" are part of Marx's appropriation of Kantian thought, we have still to bear in mind that this appropriation was not a simple and direct acquisition; it took a tremendous philosophical effort.

As is well known, Marx receives Kant's philosophy after its dynamization by Hegel. Furthermore, Kant's philosophy does not only understand itself as the final word on the conditions for the possibility of knowing, but also of doing and being. In other words, Kant believed that he had brought into the open the ultimate conditions of theory, praxis and ontology through the various critiques that he wrote. I would like to underline, at this point, that I have, in my sketch of Kant's thought, focussed on his "Critique of Pure Reason", i.e. his critique of theory; I have left out his "Critique of Practical Reason" and his "Critique of Judgement". I think that focusing on "Pure Reason" is sufficient here, where the main concern is the clarification of a minimum number of concepts relevant for an understanding of Marx's thought.

While the Kantian explication of the ultimate conditions of theory (and also of praxis and ontology) has been understood by Hegel as a puzzling proposition of a-historicity which he eventually dissolved, it is nonetheless instructive to bear in mind that this a-historicity was not the trigger of Hegel's critique of Kant. The departure point of Hegel's critique lies within a single statement of Kant's "Critique of Pure Reason" that Hegel cannot understand, were he to adhere to Kant's position.

Hegel had followed Kant's reasoning on the twelve categories faithfully and had understood Kant's claim to their a-priori-status. But then Hegel has to note, with complete disbelief that Kant grounds

---

[9]See MEW, XXIII, 192, 198, 528; XXV, 782ff; EB I, 544.

his twelve categories in twelve types of empirical judgements. This is for Hegel "...a strange science, an irrational understanding (*Erkenntnis*) of the rational" (*des Rationellen*)[10]. Kant grounds what facilitates all empirical knowledge in empirical knowledge! Out of a determinate negation of this kind of internal contradiction within Kant's thought, Hegel comes to propose his dialectics.

The determinate negation of fundamental contradictions in Kant's thought does not imply that Hegel's critique simply abolishes Kant's philosophy; it builds on it by transcending-and-containing (aufheben) it. Hegel contains Kant's subjective Idealism as he transcends it by making the subject-object-relationship dynamic. He does that by stressing the dialectic relationship between mind and matter which after all is not just absent from Kant's thought, but is conceived as being static. It is part of Hegel's Idealism that he too assigns primary status to the mind as the agent of knowledge production. Matter becomes the antithesis for the mind which is the thesis in this dialectic[11]. Knowledge as the product of the interaction between mind and matter is then still viewed as the synthesis of the two.

Hegel's determinate negation of fundamental positions in Kant's thought turns into a positive counterproposal (or determinate affirmation) to Kant's philosophy when Hegel points out that investigations into the "conditions for the possibility of knowledge to

---

[10]Quoted in Reich, Klaus: *Die Vollständigkeit der kantischen Urteilstafel*, Berlin 1932, 41.

[11]Describing the basics of Hegel's Philosophy this way is, of course, an enormous simplification. Moreover, it would be an illusion to believe that one could compensate for that simplification by a short footnote. But, in the particular connection of the mind-matter-relationship as presented by Hegel in his "*Phänomenologie*", one should at least mention that the antithesis for the mind is for Hegel, not matter or, shall we say, matter-in-itself. The antithesis rather is the mental image of matter. The world as we know it, as we have it in our mind, is the object of the human subject, whereby the latter is understood as being primarily the mind. This in a way, indicates better the modality of Hegel's Idealism. Regarding this, see also Marx's critique of Hegel in "The Holy Family" in MEW, II, in particular 89f, 177, 203f.

be" (Kant) come about only after human beings have put their investigative minds to work. Hegel observes that Newton's mechanics came prior to what Kant found out as being the conceptual conditions for the accomplishments of this physicist. Kant followed Newton's explanations and then implied that a critical inspection of Newton's mechanics would reveal the categorical make-up of the human mind.

It should be remembered that Hegel does not say that Kant was wrong in regard to the results of his philosophical inspection of Newton's work. The twelve categories indeed do underlie Newton's physics, but Kant, according to Hegel, ignores, firstly that Newton did not begin with Kant's philosophical findings when developing his mechanics and, secondly that Newton's physics is a conceptualization of nature that is historically unique and was preceded by other ways of knowing nature.

Hegel generalizes from here by saying that people do not start out in their knowledge formation with what has logical primacy, namely the categorical frame of mind; they simply apply their mind "as is" in creating knowledge. It comes later that they take reason to investigate how their minds are made up, i.e. what its "categories" are. In other words: people are not philosophers first, but doers. And yet it is out of this awareness that Hegel appreciates what Kant had done in his philosophy: he had looked at a thought, in this case Newton's physics, that was there already and had unearthed its foundations. Newton, on his part and as "a doer" did not focus on this foundation, he simply used it, and had no problems with doing that.

Hegel, therefore, proposes to look at the mind as it happens to work in any given historical situation. He proposes to study the mind as it gathers empirical knowledge in the praxis of life. Involved in that activity, the mind, however, may come across phenomena that it cannot come to terms with on the basis of assumptions or categories implicitly applied so far. The mind's accustomed ways of making sense begin to prove inadequate; thus the mind enters a state of crisis, so Hegel assumes, and therefore, is triggered to turn back onto itself. People "look over their own shoulder"; they go into reflexion and try to understand themselves[12]. In the course of this reflexion, the reason for the inadequacy of the mind will eventually be discovered. Questioning one's mind leads to self-critique. In this process, the mind gains consciousness of itself and its falsity. It should be noted that, for Hegel, the awareness of false consciousness introduces the will to overcome the limitations of the hitherto existing ways of making sense. Introducing the will to change is, of course, a broadening of Kant's concept of spontaneity, now bent back onto the revision of categories and not just on their application. Kant, as is well known, never considered the need for spontaneity to aim at a revision of the categories. History, however, forces human beings not only to bring categories so far applied into the open, it also forces human beings to change them.

In this revision, the internal problems of a mind-set are identified and determinately negated. The positive proposal of new assumptions, or new categories, that comes out of self-critique, completes the revolutionary change of the mind. The new way of making sense is more comprehensive, i.e. it can incorporate new phenomena and explain them; it is therefore, for Hegel, more abstract. The mind is now capable of making a new body of synthetic statements, in which the old ones, however, are not merely abolished but transcended-and-contained (***aufgehoben***), although in a changed form. Tracing the development of human thought through successive processes of crises and critiques turns Hegel's Dialectical Idealism into a philosophy of history.

Besides pointing out the apparent significance of such concepts like crisis, reflexion, consciousness, abstraction and revolution for Hegel's philosophy, we should also note the optimism manifest in Hegel's Idealism, not the least since it spills over into Marx's thought. Does it not come as a surprise to us how unquestioningly Hegel assumes that people try to uncover, admit and overcome internal problems of their minds? Are we today not much more aware of the possibility that people try to retain a consciousness or ways of

---

[12]See Hegel's remarks in the Introduction to his "*Grundlinien der Philosophie des Rechts*", in: Hegel, *Werke*, VII, 7.

making sense although they have ample reason to see its falsity? Being aware of the falsity of one's consciousness is for Hegel, and also for Marx, an undoubted reason for rectification. Yet Hegel's optimism goes even further than that.

He had thought that history, through a long process of crises and critiques, could arrive finally at a stage of Absolute Knowledge. At that stage, the mind and its object, the world out there, would have arrived at full identity. Mind and matter would not be alien to one another anymore. That stage would also embody the arrival of ultimate freedom. Absolute Knowledge and thus freedom would manifest themselves in such objectifications of the mind as expressed, in his time, in the Ideas of Science, Art and also in those of the State and its Law. In order to understand Hegel's reasoning, we have to remember what spontaneity of the mind has meant in that tradition.

As we have seen in the brief presentation of Kant's and Hegel's thought, spontaneity is the driving force "behind" our mind's categories. It is an automatic force, i.e. it sets itself into motion; its initial self-activation is not under our control. Of course, we can prevent ourselves from coming to know by ignoring whatever we choose to ignore. This brings to light yet another dimension of false consciousness: it comes into being where the natural drive to know and to establish clarity is hindered. It needs to be emphasized that a limitation of spontaneity is at any rate a process that takes place inside the person, regardless of whether it is a reaction to an external threat or not. If and when this limitation occurs, our spontaneity is kept from going its natural course. Freedom is absent, the self cannot realize itself; people are alienated from their true selves and live under false consciousness. Whatever else may have to be said about Absolute Knowledge, - and it is certainly a lot -, it should be clear that for Hegel dispelling darkness and having full mental clarity means freedom, since one's spontaneity feels at home in the knowledge it has helped to create. Where knowledge has arrived at an ultimate level, ultimate freedom prevails.

Marx, in his studies of Hegel's philosophy, understands that freedom is the unfolding of spontaneity. He goes along with the idealists in saying that it takes a will to know and that it also takes an unbent will to know the norms and to accept them if one is to follow them. It should, however, be pointed out that Marx unifies the human subject "behind" the theoretical reason with that "behind" the practical reason to a much greater extent than Kant in particular or Hegel have done. In fact, it has often been said that the human subject is hopelessly split between Kant's theoretical and his practical critique. For Marx, however, it is this split that causes him difficulties. For him, spontaneity cannot be relegated to the theoretical reason alone; it is immanent to practical i.e. ethical reason as well.

It is at this juncture that Marx comes to see a deep rooted contradiction within Idealism. He sees that contradiction within Hegel's views of the bureaucracy and of the philosophy of law and the state in general. When Hegel demands that the prescriptions of the legal-bureaucratic order are to be followed by the bureaucrat, then this would imply that the bureaucrat, according to Hegel, follows the universally binding logic of the law willingly (after the arrival of Absolute Knowledge). And yet, Hegel expects also that the bureaucrat would put his own self-interest aside. Does this expectation not imply that there could still be a self-interest in the bureaucrat that is not transcended-and-contained (aufgehoben) in the bureaucrat's acceptance of the legal order? Would this expectation not be a contradiction under the postulated conditions of Absolute Knowledge? Marx sees the need of expressing this expectation, even on Hegel's own terms, as a possible persistence of alienation, false consciousness and absence of freedom. To say the least, it implies an indeterminacy of spontaneity. It would mean at least a partial negation of the will in the enactment of legal prescriptions. While, on the other hand, the will would still be required for the obviously necessary understanding of these legal prescriptions and the law in general[13].

---

[13]Regarding Marx's understanding of how the individual with his/her will is to be contained in society in freedom, see his "Critique of Hegel's Philosophy of Right", MEW I, 231, 247, 273 in particular. This idea of Marx's goes back to his *Abituraufsatz*, see MEW, EB I, 594; see also MEW III, 62ff, 311f.

For Marx, this inconsistency in Hegel's Dialectical Idealism arises out of a problematic assumption in Hegel's considerations: the primacy of the cognizing mind[14]. Where such primacy is advocated, Hegel's problem becomes unavoidable; spontaneity is truncated and remains, at least in part, unaccounted for. Marx sees only one way out of the dilemma: to determinately negate the primacy of the mind. This negation implied, for Marx, the affirmation of the primacy of matter. Therefore, Marx corrects Hegel's fundamental dialectic of mind as the thesis and of matter as the antithesis by proposing to see matter as the thesis and the total human being, not just his/her mind or categorical aspect, as the antithesis. The body of the human being is not just a mere "substrate" for his/her thinking, but is constitutive for it. Only this way can one hope to account for spontaneity, and thus for the working of the mind.

Although it is well known how much Marx became influenced at that time by the Materialist teachings of Feuerbach, we have to note that he did not just oppose Hegel's Idealism with the flatly opposite Materialism of Feuerbach. Marx appreciated the dynamics of Hegel's dialectics, but he came to understand the whole human being in its concreteness, and not just its mind, as the agent of history. This way, Marx's Dialectical Materialism has transcended-and-contained (***aufgehoben***) Hegel's and Feuerbach's philosophies. This "*Aufhebung*" (transcendence-and-containment) entails the affirmation that man as the Transcending Other to Nature is the true antithesis to Nature as the thesis. Man's Otherness to Nature lies for Marx in man's spirituality. This spirituality is always more than raw nature, and yet Marx appreciates that this spirituality can never leave behind what is constitutive for it: Nature. To be clear, the peculiar feature of the human spirituality that sets it apart from the spirituality of the rest of nature is that it is capable of self-reflexion and self-critique. These mental abilities themselves remain at any given moment part of nature. It is in this sense that transcendence of nature by Other

---

[14]MEW I, 266; II, 177, 203; EB I, 572ff, 580f.

Nature does not leave nature behind[15].

In Marx's Dialectical Materialism, nature (or matter) is the overarching commonality (*das Übergreifende*) between nature and Other Nature (the Human Being). This is to say that Hegel's Idealism with its conceptualization of the mind-matter-dialectic and its mediation of a logical structure between mind and matter is transcended-and-contained in a Nature/Other-Nature Dialectic and its mediation by matter between nature and the Human Being. "Logical structure" as a mentalistic mediation is transcended-and-contained in the orderliness of nature which is, on the part of the Human Being transcended-and-contained in a conscious awareness of its own inner nature and of nature out there. The synthesis of mind and matter a la Hegel, was knowledge; now it turns, for Marx, into the synthesis between Nature and Other Nature in the form of production, i.e. the mindful and thus orderly making of material things[16]. We could visualize this dialectic in the following way (N = nature, ON = other nature or human being, P = production):

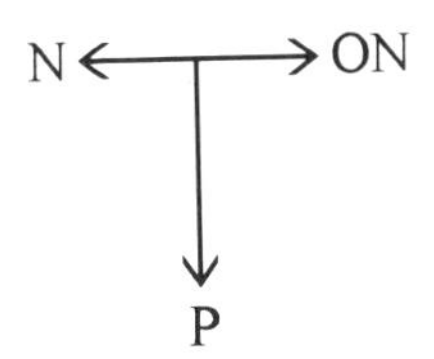

Having arrived at this point in his considerations, Marx knows that he can no longer be just a philosopher of man's mental activities. His philosophy demands on its own grounds the inclusion of the material concrete activities of the human subjects by seeing the latter in their own material concreteness. Not doing that would mean to

---

[15]See MEW II, 49, 147, 188ff; III, 6, 31, 41f, 237f; XXIII, 57f, 192, 528ff; EB I, 516ff, 539ff, 558, 578f, 591.

[16]MEW III, 20f; XIX, 2; XXIII, 192, 198, 281f; EB I, 471-83, 512ff, 515ff, 574; "*Grundrisse*", 585-99. (See also the references in footnote 18).

betray not only his own thoughts but also those of his philosophical predecessors to the extent that they have been changed through their transcendence-and-containment in his own appropriation. In this sense, Dialectical Materialism is a faithful continuation of the Critical Tradition of German Philosophy.

Focusing, from then on, his attention firmly on the materially concrete activities of human beings implies for Marx that he has to study Political Economy. He knows that he has to study the production of things and their exchange in their totality; neither commerce, engineering, manufacturing or the study of balance sheets of individual entrepreneurs can be the segregated *foci* of his attention; as merely isolated aspects of a whole, they would only allow for decontextualized, i.e. distorted judgements. This is to say then that Marx becomes a philosopher of economics[17]; he knows that he has to deliver a Critique of Political Economy. But by no stretch of the imagination does this mean that he changes from being a philosopher to being an economist or, worse yet, as some say, an economic determinist. Would the latter kind of a criticism not suffer from a misunderstanding of Marx's concepts of spontaneity and dialectics? How could a determinist ever propose to change reality if the latter had determinate power? Marx remains a philosopher, but one who wishes not only to understand the praxis of his times, but also to change it on that occasion, as he has said in the eleventh Thesis on Feuerbach.

Studying the economic order of his time and place (and ultimately not more, as we shall see), he understands that production takes place in a specific social form: labor[18] is carried out by using the means of production as they are provided by capital[19]. Marx understands labor

---

[17]If so, then certainly not in Proudhon's sense! See Marx's "The Misery of Philosophy", MEW IV, 63-182 (especially chapter 2: "The Metaphysics of Political Economy").

[18]MEW II, 37; III, 33; IV, 475f, XXIII, 511ff; EB I, 473f, 529. (See also the references in footnotes 16 and 19).

[19]MEW XXIII, 247, 328f; EB I, 483-97. (See also the references in footnotes 16 and 18).

and capital as forces of production which are to be distinguished from the means of production (like tools, agricultural land, raw material, etc.). These forces of production, Marx notes, stand also in a dialectical relationship. Here, the logical primacy goes to labor; it is the thesis in this dialectic, while capital, i.e. the accumulated surplus accruing from labor, is its transcending other, i.e. the antithesis to labor. Thus labor and capital form the relations of production, as they create, or synthesize themselves in, the material base of society. The following may be an adequate visualization of this now enlarged dialectical edifice (L = labor, C = capital, B = basis):

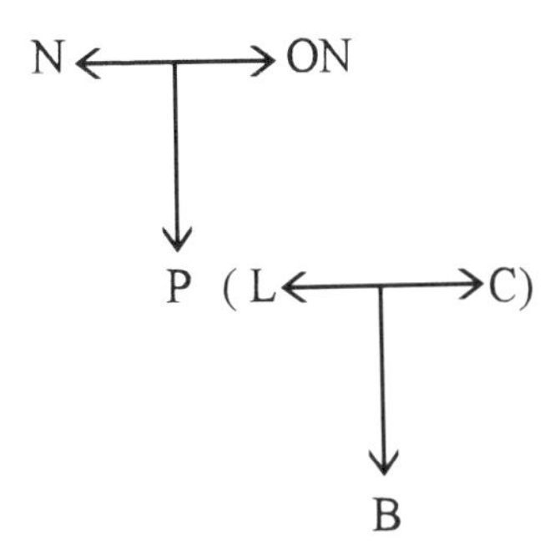

The workings of the material basis of society are, of course, not a mindless functioning; society is not seen by Marx as a machine or as a cybernetic system as we might say today. "Behind" all the materially concrete activities of society is a meaning in terms of which the totality of all phenomena is understood, evaluated and/or normatively regulated. These cultural aspects of society are referred to by Marx as the superstructure; it constitutes the transcending other to the material basis[20]. This cluster of meanings, norms and values is, in the language of Marx's philosophical predecessors, the totality of the synthetic judgements possible and at work in society. In Marx's

---

[20]Regarding the notions of "economic base" and "superstructure" and the relation between the two, see MEW I, 386, 354f, 597; II, 85, 128; III, 13ff, 21, 26ff, 31, 37f, 46f, 62, 71f, 128, 227, 233, 405, 480f, 539; IV, 130, 134f, 480; XIII, 7ff, 409; EB I, 537.

own terms, we could say that the dialectic between basis and superstructure synthesizes itself in the totality of the capitalist mode of production. Again, I would like to visualize this (SS = superstructure):

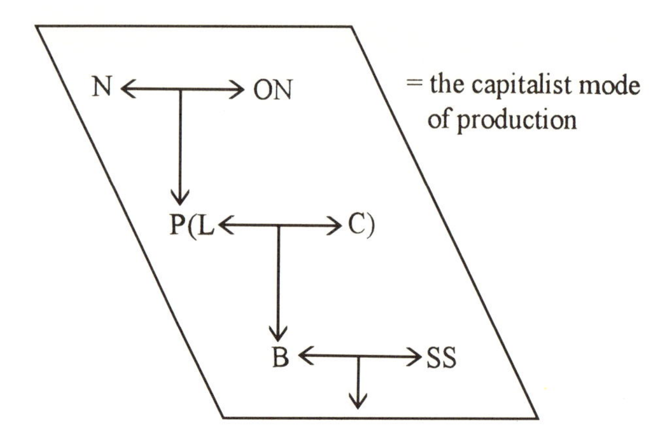

At this juncture, it would seem to be appropriate to underline the difference between Marx as a philosopher of praxis and all hitherto existing philosophies as philosophies of the mind, i.e. of ideas and theories. Marx's Critique of Political Economy is not only different from previous critiques because of the object that it concerns itself with, but also because Marx's critique discovers a materially-concrete contradiction in the object of his understanding. The materially-concrete contradiction is practised in the labor-capital relationship insofar as it implies mutual destruction, obviously first that of labor and then, consequentially, that of capital. This concrete contradiction does not only imply a concrete contradiction between nature and the human being, i.e. between Nature and Other Nature in the sense that we make nature uninhabitable for us, but it also implies the mental contradiction between economic basis and superstructure. In other words, Marx is aware of the philosophical and the practical implications (in the traditional sense of the words) of our praxis for our theory. This is to say that Marx's Philosophy of

Economics transcends-and-contains the philosophy of his predecessors[21].

Dwelling for a moment on the superstructural aspects of the capitalist mode of production, it seems to be opportune to discuss two issues about which there exists a good deal of confusion.

One can approach the first of these issues by appreciating that the superstructure as the transcending other to the economic basis is certainly an aspect in which work has to be done as well, and not only in the labor-capital-interaction. Culture requires work in schools, in courts of law, concert halls, churches, even in families. All these activities are required as well for the survival of the society given its capitalist structure. This is not the least of the reasons for which Marx says that all social relations are economic relations. Of course, Marx speaks here as a Political Economist and not in terms of an economics that has imploded to a concern for the individuated profit motive only. Marx, therefore, must not be interpreted as if he had intended to say that all social relations were meant to yield a profit like the labor-capital-relation. To understand Marx in the latter way reveals one's individualistic outlook on life and thus one's inability to grasp Marx's sense for man's "communist essence".

The second issue relates to the claim that Dialectical Materialism is universally applicable. Rectification of this misunderstanding is more difficult, since Marx himself was not always clear on this matter.

I think it needs to be born in mind that his Critique of Political Economy was geared to the theory and praxis, i.e. to the superstructure and the material basis of Capitalism, as they existed in his time and place. This already implies that his own work,

---

[21]On occasion, Marx speaks of the *forces of production* and the relations between them as the "material conditions to blow up bourgeois society"; see e.g. "*Grundrisse*" 593f. Regarding contradictions and crises in Capitalism, see also MEW VII, 97f; IX, 101.

undoubtedly a theoretical endeavor itself, was relative to a particular moment in history and not to history in general[22].

On the other hand, it can certainly not be denied that Marx, particularly in his younger years, did make claims to the general applicability of his thought. Everybody knows, for instance, the opening sentence of the Communist Manifesto of 1848: "The history of all hitherto existing societies is the history of class struggles". In later years, however, at the latest in the English edition of 1888, this sentence is accompanied by a footnote in which Engels raises the question as to what one should do about those societies that did not have classes. Is this not, in effect, a withdrawal of the claim to generality?

Besides, it might be even more informative to listen to what Karl Marx has said himself on the generality of his critique. In a letter, written in 1877 to a Russian journal he objects to those who "...metamorphose my historical sketch of the genesis of capitalism in Western Europe into an historico-philosophical theory of the general path every people is fated to tread". In the same letter, he also says that an understanding of the particular will never be accomplished "...by using, as one's master key, a general historico-philosophical theory, the supreme virtue of which consists in being super-historical"[23].

---

[22]The relativity of thought to, or the groundedness of thought in the material basis has been a matter of awareness for Marx throughout his life (his earlier claims to the general applicability of his own thought notwithstanding). See e.g. MEW, III, 5; IV, 130, 140, 483f; XIX, 401f. (See also the references in footnote 23).

[23]MEW, XIX, 111f. In this connection, I would like to remind the reader of footnote 6. We have learned there that Marx had his reason not to retain the "Introduction" to the "*Grundrisse*" in later drafts of "The Capital" or in "The Capital" itself. Obviously, Marx objected already as early as 1859 against formulating what could be understood as a general theoretical framework for the study of the concrete. This is to say that his suggestion to start in the course of social studies with the concrete was not intended as a theoretical methodological proposition of a "superhistorical" kind. Such a proposition could too easily be misunderstood as an attempt to replace the primacy of matter by the *concept* of the primacy of matter.

Furthermore, a claim to generality on the part of Dialectical Materialism would imply a fatal internal contradiction in its logic. If Dialectical Materialism were to be used as a pre-established conceptual framework for the comprehension of a particular circumstance and its own materially-concrete aspects, then it would assume the status of logical primacy for the mind, i.e. it would contradict its initial insight, i.e. that into the primacy of matter. This dilemma could only be resolved by either determinately negating the primacy of matter or by demonstrating that the primacy of matter is also contained in the symbolic realm. The latter, of course, could not be done by merely philosophizing about it, but by living that containment.

Finally we have to note that Marx's concept of understanding excludes an idealist and generalist interpretation of Dialectic Materialism. This comes out with all the desirable clarity in a long statement included in the "Introduction" to the "*Grundrisse*". It appears there under the title of "The Method of Political Economy". While I have to postpone a closer inspection of that important passage once we get to the commentary on that "Introduction", we have to note, already in the present connection, that Marx objects there to an imposition of any prefabricated thought on the study of any local circumstance. He emphatically rejects such an attempt as a distortion of the locally-concrete reality under consideration, and says that only a Hegelian would engage in it.

On the other hand, not imposing one's own abstractions does not imply, for Marx, the uncritical acceptance of the abstractions that people to be understood have about themselves. Doing this would

---

Nothing was further from his mind than such a Hegelian idea.

Besides referring the reader back to pp.xf of my text, it may also be instructive to return to MEW, XIX, 401f as referred to in footnote 22. This reference is taken from Marx's exchange of 1881 with Vera Zasulitsch about the Russian rural community. Marx does not only repeatedly limit his ideas to the West on this occasion (see e.g. the first two paragraphs of that communication), he also speaks of his thoughts on Capitalism as a "so-called theory" (see the beginning of the section titled "Concept III" in this exchange with V. Zasulitsch).

simply mean a reversal of the "Hegelian" position, in the sense that primacy would not be given to the philosopher's mind, but to that of the people instead. Nonetheless, Hegel's awareness of the involvement of reflexion, critique, negation, etc. in the process of learning is not lost in Marx's Materialism, regardless of how much the latter is additionally informed by the primacy of matter. This way, Marx's concept of false consciousness takes on a dimension that transcends-and-contains what Hegel understood by it. Inspecting this briefly gives me the opportunity to also discuss the concept of ideology.

Marx was well aware of the possibility that the thinking claimed to be "behind" the economic basis of a society may in fact not be "behind" it at all. This may, for instance, come into the open, when a researcher tries to understand a society. The sense that a people claims to make may be unacceptable for him, because of the contradictions within that sense and/or between it and its economic basis. While trying to make the sense that Capitalism claims to make about itself, Marx found out that the theoretical writings, i.e. the capitalist self-explanations, were riddled with contradictions. We will have ample opportunity to see this later in this study. At least since the time that he had come to understand the nature of surplus value and of exploitation, i.e. since the forties of the last century[24], Marx knew that the theories of Capitalism that did not spell out the materially concrete contradiction between labor and capital, have to lie about the meaning of Capitalism. Capitalism requires a superstructure that both veils the material contradictions of

---

[24]Marx's first publication in which he focuses on economic matters appeared under the title of "*Lohnarbeit und Kapital*" ("Wage Labor and Capital") in the "*Neue Rheinische Zeitung*" between the 5th and the 11th of April 1849. This is not to deny, of course, that already his "The Misery of Philosophy", first published in 1847, contained long passages related to economic matters as did his "Economic-Philosophical Manuscripts" of 1844 (which, however, remained unpublished at that time). A short sketch of Marx's intellectual move into the realm of Political Economy can be found in his "Preface" to "*Zur Kritik der Politischen Okonomie*" written in January 1859 in London, see MEW XIII, 3ff.

Capitalism and, in doing so, turns that self-explanation into mere ideology; it is not and cannot be true[25].

Another aspect of ideology comes to light when one examines the status of Christianity in the capitalist mode of production. A good many people make the claim that their daily life is guided by Christian teachings, although the expectation of "Love thy Neighbor" cannot possibly be reconciled with the capitalist praxis of competition. Capitalism, on its part, cannot be without competition; it is intrinsic to it. It could, therefore, be said that Christianity is as little as the capitalist self-explanation the superstructure "behind" and involved in the capitalist praxis. Christianity too is a mere ideology for it[26].

The example of Christianity, although not intrinsic to Capitalism, demonstrates that an ideology fulfills a purpose in the capitalist mode of production. If nothing else, Christianity like other ideologies, serves as an opiate for the people in sustaining false consciousness[27]. In addition, it has to be borne in mind that ideology is something different for those who hand it out and for those supposed to accept it. And yet, it signifies, at any rate, alienation[28] from true consciousness. Obviously though, the capitalist has little reason to do away with his false consciousness, because he stands to gain from its perpetuation. But the proletariat was expected by Marx to cut the veil of ideology, simply because, so Marx thought, that the misery of the proletariat would allow the proletariat to understand the materially contradictory relation between capital and labor. The proletariat would understand that the "tendentially falling rate of profit" would lead to an ever increasing rate of the exploitation of labor. Marx expected that the proletariat would thus liberate itself

---

[25]Regarding ideology, see: MEW I, 68,281, 294f, 345, 352ff, 378f, 575; II, 85f, 128; III, (i.e. "The German *Ideology*) 26f, 30ff, 37ff, 46f, 143, 167, 227f, 233, 405, 480f; IV, 130, 477ff, 480; VIII, 139f; IX, 225; XXVII, 409; EB I, 262f, 371f.

[26]MEW I, 352, 374ff, 378, 385, 579; III, 26f, 31f, 120, 143; IV, 480.

[27]MEW I, 579; II, 55f; III, 31f.

[28]MEW EB I, 537, 542f (see also references in footnote 29).

from false consciousness, ideology and the system that inflicts the misery and the confusion, namely the capitalist mode of production. This way, the proletariat would not only be a class in itself, but it would become a class for itself.

The concept and the expectation of this Revolution was Marx's response to Hegel's idea on the philosophy of history. The difference, though, is that Marx has moved gradually away from using that concept for the understanding of all history - the first sentence of the Communist Manifesto notwithstanding - towards the making of history at a particular point in time and space, i.e. in the capitalist West. Marx's concept of Revolution looks forward and suggests the conscious and practical shaping of the future so that true history can begin. Marx thus transcends-and-contains Hegel's concept of revolution in two ways: it is no longer backwards oriented, i.e. projected into the past, and it is not thought of as bringing about history's end on the occasion of arriving at a classless society. This also means that "classless society" is not Marx's equivalent for Hegel's Absolute Knowledge[29]. Instead Marx's concept of Revolution opens a door for a conscious continuation of history into the future, and thus transcends-and-contains the Hegelian finiteness of theory and praxis.

There is hardly any indication in Marx's writings that he feared that the Revolution would not occur in the near future. This reveals an optimism that he shares, mutatis mutandis, with his philosophical predecessors. I think that, among other aspects, this optimism alone would call for a renewed attempt at understanding his way of thinking. The question would be, why is Marx so sure that human beings want clarity and want to rectify the wrongs of their praxis?

It must be admitted that Marx does not give an explicit answer to this question of ours in the "Introduction" to the "*Grundrisse*". But, I do believe that his way of thinking, can be gleaned to some extent from these pages to which I would like to turn my attention now, and

---

[29]MEW II, 89f, 177, 203, 266; IV, 125ff (Hegel's method is only implied here); EB I, 571f, 574f, 580f.

that their reading may invite one or the other person to further studies of Marx's mind so that the reason for his optimism may become clear.

At this juncture, it may be appropriate to point out that the text of the "Introduction" may quite often bring up considerations to the contemporary mind which Marx could not possibly have foreseen. Usually, although always tempted, I have left the contemplation on the implications of Marx's statements for today's political economy to the reader.

Part II

A Commentary on the "Introduction" to the "*Grundrisse*"

1.- Individuation and Generality: Bourgeois Abstractions

The first excerpt that I think should be looked at is taken from page 83 of the English translation of the "Introduction".

> The individual and isolated hunter and fisherman, with whom Smith and Ricardo begin, belongs among the unimaginative conceits of the eighteenth-century Robinsonades... It is, rather, the anticipation of 'civil society', in preparation since the sixteenth century and making giant strides towards maturity in the eighteenth. In this society of free competition, the individual appears detached from the natural bonds etc. which in earlier historical periods makes him the accessory of a definite and limited human conglomerate. Smith and Ricardo still stand with both feet on the shoulders of the eighteenth-century prophets, in whose imaginations this eighteenth-century individual - the product on one side of the dissolution of the feudal forms of society, on the other side of the new forces of production developed since the sixteenth

> century - appears as an ideal, whose existence they project into the past. Not as a historic result but as history's point of departure. As the Natural Individual appropriate to their notion of human nature, not arising historically, but posited by nature.

Marx discusses here an assumption usually made in 18th century Political Economy, for instance, by Adam Smith and David Ricardo. The assumption is that the isolated individual had been in existence since the dawn of history, although it was merely an ideal posited by the 18th century theories. This ideal became concrete reality when it emerged in the praxis of civil society, meaning here, in capitalist society. Making this assumption, Political Economists lose sight of the circumstance that the isolated individual which they take to be nature-given is only a particular form of social existence and a historically late one at that. Different from earlier historical periods, the individual today (i.e. during Capitalism) lives in free competition by appearing to be detached from the natural social bonds in which he/she was embedded while living in definitely circumscribed social associations. This indicates that Marx sees the detached individual as the product of the historical process of a gradually increasing individuation. That product can only be projected into the past at the cost of not only confusing one's understanding of the past, but also of the present as a historically peculiar phenomenon[30].

The concept of individuation receives further attention in the next excerpt:

p.84 Only in the eighteenth century, in 'civil society', do the various forms of social connectedness confront the individual as a mere means towards his private purposes, as external necessity. But the epoch which produces this

---

[30]MEW I, 368ff (bourgeois individuation seen as a product of history); II, 127f; III, 54f; XIX, 403f (focusing on the process of individuation through the development of private property rights in agricultural land); EB I, 557, 594.

> standpoint, that of the isolated individual, is also precisely that of the hitherto most developed social (from this standpoint, general) relations. The human being is in the most literal sense a *zoon politicon*, not merely a gregarious animal, but an animal which can individuate itself only in the midst of society. Production by an isolated individual outside society...is as much of an absurdity as is the development of language without individuals living *together* and talking to each other. There is no point in dwelling on this any longer. The point could go entirely unmentioned if this twaddle...had not been earnestly pulled back into the centre of the most modern economics by Bastiat, Carey, Proudhon etc. (Marx's italics, FWS).

Here, the inspection of the end result of the historical process of individuation is carried further in, altogether, three directions:

First, Marx notes that the individual of civil society, i.e. of free competition, sees, or is confronted by, social relations as mere means to his/her individual or private ends. This thought was later on developed by Max Weber in his "debate with Marx's ghost", into the concept of rationalism, i.e. that of individuated means-ends-thinking (as contrasted by Weber to social means-ends-thinking, i.e. rationality).

Second, the "standpoint" of the "isolated individual" can only be produced in the midst of the socially most developed society so far, i.e. in the society with the most complex social relations, namely in civil society. And yet, considering oneself as being an isolated individual is merely a standpoint, i.e. a way of seeing which does not only not do away with the reality of the "social connectedness" but, this standpoint in its falsity, also precludes the awareness that it is only in the midst of modern social relations that the individual can individuate him/herself and can, therefore, enact his/her political essence, i.e. his/her directedness toward the totality of society. The confusion in not seeing that individuation and sociality imply one another is illustrated by Marx's reference to language. The development of language requires a form of individuality that remains open to all others. To theorize about social relations in any other way, as Capitalism misleads one to do, is absurd. "There is no point in dwelling on this any longer". And yet, Marx has discussed this "twaddle", since it is not only practiced in Capitalism but also because it is being propagated by the economic theories of Bastiat, Carey and Proudhon.

Third, and this is already contained in the previous point, the contradiction within (or absurdity of) the modern standpoint points beyond itself in the form of a "determinate negation". Robinsonades have to be transcended-and-contained by a praxis and theory that live the social, or better yet, the political nature of economics and being.

What Marx has done so far in this text boils down to a critique and rejection of any attempt at proposing a historically particular state in individuation as the reference point for the study of all modes of production. In the next set of excerpts, Marx discusses, in a perhaps at first puzzling way, the concept of the general aspects and/or preconditions of production.

p.85 *Production in general* is an abstraction, but a rational abstraction in so far as it really brings out and fixes the common element and thus saves us repetition. Still, this *general* category, this common element sifted out by comparison, is itself segmented many times over and splits into different determinations. Some determinations belong to all epochs, others only to a few. [Some] determinations will be shared by the most modern epoch and the most ancient. No production will be thinkable without them; however, even though the most developed languages have laws and characteristics in common with the least developed, nevertheless, just those things which determine their development, i.e. the elements which are not general and common, must be separated out from the determinations valid for production as such, so that in their unity - which arises already from the identity of the subject, humanity, and of the object, nature - their essential difference is not forgotten. The whole profundity of those modern economists who demonstrate the eternity and harmoniousness of the existing social relations lies in this

> forgetting. For example. No production possible without an instrument of production, even if this instrument is only the hand. No production without stored-up, past labour, p.86 even if it is only the facility//gathered together and concentrated in the hand of the savage by repeated practice. Capital is, among other things, also an instrument of production, also objectified, past labour. Therefore capital is general, eternal relation of nature; that is, if I leave out just the specific quality which alone makes 'instrument of production' and 'stored-up labour' into capital. The entire history of production relations thus appears to Carey, for example, as malicious forgery perpetrated by governments (Marx's italics, FWS).

To begin with, it is quite unfortunate that, in the second section of this excerpt, the translation uses the phrase "general category". The problem lies with the word "category". That word has a distinct meaning among Critical Philosophers, as we saw above, and that meaning is not intended here. Moreover, the equivalent word "*Kategorie*" is not used in the German original. There, only the equivalent word for "general" is used, but it is transformed into a noun; it reads there "***dies Allgemeine***". I am not sure whether translating it with the phrase "that which is general" would have been too awkward in English, but it would probably not have confused the kind of reader who would normally study this text.

Regarding the first sentence of this excerpt, we have to bear in mind the historical dynamics which Hegel implied when he used the word abstraction[31]. Each level of history had its own abstractions which rested for Hegel with a particular categorical make-up of the human mind. While Marx dissolves, in his critique of Hegel, the idea of Absolute Knowledge, the idea of an absolute abstraction, i.e. a final set of categories, vanishes as well. According to Marx, we are left with only historically (and, locally, as we shall see later), valid

---

[31]See for Marx's dealings with this MEW I, 232ff, 313; II, 60ff.

abstractions; a Hegelian absolute abstraction is out of the question for him.

And yet, Marx does not deny that there is a measure of usefulness to an abstraction like "production in general", since it allows one to bring out common elements of different forms of production and "thus saves us repetition". Abstractions in that sense facilitate communication. There are, however, serious problems with abstractions like "generality". The generality thought of here, ignores for instance, that forms of production are composed of many features, i.e. that each one of them "is segmented many times" and "into different determinants". Not all of them may be present in any given form of production, or some of the essential features of production may appear in it in different forms. As an example Marx refers, besides the differences among languages which still have characteristic features in common, to the differences in the instruments of production. The human hand, with the skills ("facility") gathered in it, and capital, with "objectified, past labor" gathered in that are both instruments of production. But a study which would subsume both of them under the same general concept of "instrument of production" would be in the danger of leaving out the essential and yet different qualities of each of these instruments. To be sure, such a generalization could be made, in order to simplify communication in certain circumstances, but confusion could arise all too easily. It is, therefore, important to note those elements of a phenomenon, in this case those of production, which "are not general and common", but different and specific. These different specificities are essential to each form of production and to an understanding of it. They can therefore not be treated as if they were merely "a malicious forgery perpetrated by governments", as, among others, Carey had suggested. While Marx seems to be, at first, quite willing to accept "production in general" as a short-hand phrase, he moves finally away from such kindness to his intellectual opponents. The uniqueness of each mode of production is too important for him to be ignored. This already indicates what we will see later in this text with even greater clarity, namely, that it is intrinsic to Marx's thinking to abstain from "general theory construction". As we saw above, later in his life he objects to such an attempt very explicitly.

While Marx concludes this consideration by rejecting the notion of "production in general", we should also pay attention to a remark apparently made in passing in the above excerpt. This remark is quite important for Marx's way of trying to do justice to the peculiarity of any situation in terms of that situation's own immanent abstraction. More or less in the middle of the above excerpt, when he speaks of these elements of production which "are not general and common" and yet "must not be forgotten", Marx also speaks of the unity as it "arises ... from the identity of the subject, humanity, and of the object, nature". First, let us note that the German text does not use the equivalent German noun "*Identität*". It simply says that subject and object are "the same" ("*dieselben*"); in other words, both are nature. This, however, does not mean that Marx thinks of the human subject as being merely nature; we have spoken above of Marx's concept of man as Other Nature. He obviously speaks of something here that allows subject and object, human being and nature, to become a unity in each form of production, no matter how different these forms are from one another. Although there have been tremendous differences in production in the various social associations of our species, both on the subjective, conceptual and the objective, material side of production, it is still so that in each of these cases human beings and nature have managed to produce, to form a unity, i.e. to synthesize human subjectivity and nature's objectivity. This is to say, in the light of what we have explained in connection with Kant and, mutatis mutandis, Hegel, that the categories living in the subject and in the object provided both the human beings and what was nature for them, with an identity in themselves and for each other so that different forms of production as different syntheses between man and nature could take place successfully all over this world at all times[32]. But even this view does not lead Marx to suggest that we should search for a generality among all forms of production in such a way that we blur their differences and their uniqueness. In a little while we will see that Marx prefers to identify the generality (or unity) as it exists among the elements of a specific mode of production.

Marx is not only sceptical about the idea of "production in general", he also doubts the appropriateness of speaking of "general preconditions of all production". This comes out in the following excerpt which, in passing, sheds some light on Marx's concept of natural laws as well.

> p.86 It is the fashion to preface a work of economics with a general part - and precisely this part figures under the title 'production' (see for example J. St. Mill) - treating of the *general preconditions* of all production.
>
> p.87 [...//that e.g. certain races, locations, climates, natural conditions such as harbours, soil fertility, etc. are more advantageous to production than others...] the economists' real concern ... is, rather to present production - see e.g. Mill - as distinct from distribution etc., as encased in eternal natural laws independent of history, at which opportunity *bourgeois* relations are then quietly smuggled in as the inviolable natural laws on which society in the abstract is founded. This is the more or less conscious purpose of the whole proceeding. In distribution, by contrast, humanity has allegedly permitted itself to be considerably more arbitrary (Marx's italics, FWS).

---

[32]Differences in the *forms of production* imply that one cannot say that *labor* (as subjectivity) is *the* source of surplus, nor, of course, is it simply *nature*. The point is that the interaction between *labor* and *nature* creates wealth. It is intrinsic to this interaction and its two forces that they manifest themselves and their synthesis, i.e. wealth, in different *forms*. See MEW IV, 130; XIX, 15; XXV, 782ff; EB I, 515ff.

It would probably be helpful to begin our work on this excerpt with a clarification of the word distribution. Distribution as understood by Marx is to be distinguished from exchange. We could perhaps say that the concept of exchange relates to market activities, while Marx speaks of distribution in relation to investment, e.g. the distribution of funds and/or people into the various branches of production.

With this in mind, Marx notes that distribution is usually relegated by Political Economists to the sphere of history, i.e. a sphere "considerably more arbitrary" than that of production. The latter is, also for our everyday views today, more directly "encased in eternal natural laws independent of history" than distribution is. Therefore, we might tend to believe, that we could find a "general precondition of all production" in the Natural Sciences. The problem however, is that Marx does not indicate in that whole paragraph from which this excerpt is taken that he is talking about a Natural Science in our sense of the word. At best he makes reference to "natural conditions such as harbours, soil fertility etc.". Instead of talking about Physics, Chemistry and so forth, Political Economists like Mill treat production itself as if it would follow natural laws. This is for Marx the point "...at which... *bourgeois* (Marx's italics) relations are ... quietly smuggled in as the inviolable natural laws on which society in the abstract is founded."

What Marx opposes at this juncture is the *clandestine* assumption of bourgeois relations as if they could be treated as having the status of natural laws and technology. He knows that not only the knowledge that bourgeois society has about nature but also about itself (Sociology) is part of the superstructure of a mode of production, i.e. is relative to that mode of production. The point for him is *not* to conceal that. Different modes of production have different ways of knowing nature and themselves. For that reason, also the Natural Science of today would only be a historically peculiar form of such knowledge. On these grounds, Marx rejects all suggestions which refer to the generality of pre-conditions for production as being given by nature. A separation between natural laws and social order, let alone hiding the interrelation between them, does not even enter his mind. If this interrelation is hidden, as done by Mills, then this manoeuvre leads all too often to an elevation of the capitalist social laws and natural laws to the fictional status of having unchangeable validity.

It would go beyond my present task in this commentary on Marx to address the problem of today's Sciences. So much should be clear, though: A Natural Science that loses so consistently sight of one of the parts of nature, namely the human being, and a Social Science that has no adequate sense either for the nature of the human being, threaten, precisely for this reason, the survival of us as parts of nature.

At the end of Portion One of the "Introduction", Marx has this to say:

> p.88 To summarize: There are characteristics which all stages of production have in common, and which are established as general ones by the mind; but the so-called *general preconditions* of all production are nothing more than these abstract moments with which no real historical stage of production can be grasped (Marx's italics, FWS).

This short paragraph does not only say that "general preconditions" of production do not contribute to an understanding of a "real historical stage of production", it also cautions against the notion of generality as it is "established...by the mind". This prepares us perhaps for a notion of generality that is of a different kind than being merely a mental construct. The weight of Marx's objection against notions "established by the mind" will be better understood when we see him later in this "Introduction" objecting against the ways in which "the theoretical mind appropriates the world".

2.- Marx's Concept of General Relation

The summary of the first section of the "Introduction" is directly followed by Section Two of the "Introduction" which presents yet another treatment of "the general". This is how Marx begins:

p.88 THE GENERAL RELATION OF PRODUCTION TO DISTRIBUTION, EXCHANGE, CONSUMPTION

Before going further in the analysis of production, it is necessary to focus on the various categories which the economists line up next to it.

The obvious, trite notion: in production the members of society appropriate (create, shape) the products of nature in accord with human needs; distribution determines the

p.89 proportion in which the//individual shares in the product; exchange delivers the particular products into which the individual desires to convert the portion which distribution has assigned to him. And finally, in consumption, the products become objects of gratification, of individual appropriation. Production creates the objects which correspond to the given needs; distribution divides them up according to social laws; exchange further parcels out the already divided shares in accord with individual needs; and finally, in consumption, the product steps outside this social movement and becomes a direct object and servant of individual need, and satisfies it in being consumed...

Thus production, distribution, exchange and consumption form a regular syllogism; production is the generality, distribution and exchange the particularity,and consumption the singularity in which the whole is joined together. This is admittedly a coherence, but a shallow one...

The opponents of the political economists - whether inside or outside its realm - who accuse them of barbarically

> tearing apart things which belong together, stand either on the same ground as they, or beneath them. Nothing is more p.90 common than the re//proach that the political economists view production too much as an end in itself, that distribution is just as important. This accusation is based precisely on the economic notion that the spheres of distribution and of production are independent, autonomous neighbours. Or that these moments were not grasped in their unity. As if this rupture had made its way not from reality into the textbooks, but rather from the textbooks into reality, and as if the task were the dialectic balancing of concepts, and not the grasping of real relations!

Already the title of this, the second section of the "Introduction", will take many of us by great surprise. Marx seems to speak again about the generality of production which he had so vociferously rejected in Section One. Now he does not only speak of generality of production but also of that of the relations of production to distribution, exchange and consumption. This apparent contradiction calls for a careful analysis of this whole section of the "Introduction". At the end of that analysis, we will see that it does not only teach us a new concept of generality, but also guides us considerably deeper into Marx's distinct way of thinking.

Unfortunately, I have to begin with by pointing out, once again, the confusing use of the word "category", as it shows up in the first sentence of this excerpt. The German original uses the word "*Rubrik*". I do not see any reason not to translate it into the exact English equivalent, namely "rubric". Using the word "category", by ignoring its specific meaning, is misleading in the present context.

Obviously, Marx goes into this section out of the awareness, that his dealings with production so far in this "Introduction" are not sufficient. In fact, he has mainly dealt with insufficient treatments of that concept by others. As a political economist, he knows that a further analysis of production has to be carried out by viewing it in the context of distribution, exchange and consumption. Marx summarizes what economists have normally said about that relationship. However, when he speaks again of the generality of production in this summary, he indicates that he now will use the concept of generality in a very different way. Marx's study begins by admitting that there is a "regular syllogism" among these four processes. He agrees with the widespread idea that this syllogism is "a coherence", but he calls it "a shallow one". This remark is directed at two different positions at the same time: on the one hand, he shares the objection of "the opponents of the political economists ... who accuse them (the political economists, FWS) of barbarically tearing apart things (i.e. production, distribution, exchange and consumption, FWS) which belong together"; on the other hand however, he objects also against the same "opponents", because they act "as if this rupture (between production, distribution, exchange and consumption, FWS) had made its way not from reality into the textbooks, but rather from the textbooks into reality"[33]. Marx obviously implies here that reality has to be taken as the departure point for studying the question of how these four aspects of the economy are related, although the rupture among them exists already in reality. This is to say that Marx appears to advocate an empiricist approach, but he does so only in appearance and not in reality, since he indicates through his agreement with the "shallow" argument of the "opponents of the political economists" that he too cannot agree with the rupture that has been created by those practically involved in economic reality. But this is also to say that he still wishes to grasp the "real relations" and does not see "the dialectic balancing of *concepts*" (emphasis added, FWS) as his task. This is a task he likes to leave to the Hegelians.

The suggestion to take concrete reality critically as a departure point already announces, how Marx's study of political economy is a critique of both the praxis of political economy and of its theoreticians. A further unfolding of his "Method of Political Economy" comes up later, but it should be clear already that his call for trying to make sense by proceeding from reality is neither an

[33]MEW I, 384 (on the similar relationship between German Philosophy - in this case Hegel's - and German reality); III, 218, 432f, 435; EB I, 327ff.

empiricism nor an idealist attempt at "the dialectic balancing of concepts" as is so common among political economists. What is it, then, that Marx wants to tell us about the "coherence" among production, distribution, exchange and consumption? I would like to present an answer to this question, first in a summarizing fashion so that later we may be less in the danger of getting lost in the detail.

Basically, Marx announces that he wishes to focus on the "coherence" among these four aspects of the economy in terms of the identities[34] they share. These identities lie with the *form* that mediates each one of them with the others. It needs to be noted that the concept of mediation is still used here in the Kantian-Hegelian sense, but while Kant (and Hegel) related it to the explicated categories which the cognizing mind of the human subject and the world out there have in common, Marx points at the mediation as it occurs among these four aspects of the economy in themselves. In other words, for Kant, it was the human subject and the world that are mediated through the sharing of categories, while for Marx, it is the four aspects of the economy that mediate each other for themselves. An externally observing human subject and his/her subjective mind in whose understanding these mediations matter are not yet under Marx's consideration here[35]. The talk is about the "coherence" as it exists within the objective-material side of the economic process. This is how Marx avoids an idealist attempt at "a dialectical balancing of concepts". He does so by addressing the material dialectics as it occurs in the *objective processes* themselves and in what mediates them to each other[36].

---

[34]For Marx's use of this term, see MEW XIX, 363; EB I, 529, 552.

[35]The absence of an observing subject seems to express itself also in Marx's style. In the presently inspected Part Two Marx hardly ever uses the personal pronoun "I", while in Part Three, "The Method of Political Economy", the use of the personal pronoun "I" is quite frequent.

[36]Marx's project in this regard goes far beyond earlier considerations as he has presented them, e.g. in the "Economic-Philosophical Manuscripts" of 1844, see MEW EB I, 512ff, 542f or 573f; see also EB I 215ff. Only a few years later, e.g. in "The German Ideology", Marx suggests with yet greater confidence to turn to the empirical world, see e.g. MEW III, 218,

It may also be appropriate to note that Marx makes, already at this stage, passing reference to the relation between exchange and distribution. There are two short elaborations on that matter in the above excerpt. They read: 1.- "... exchange delivers the particular products into which the individual desires to convert the portion which distribution has assigned to him; ..." and 2.- "... exchange further parcels out the already divided shares in accord with individual needs;...". In both these sentences, Marx refers to exchange in relationship to individual needs and desires. This too will require closer attention later. But what is already worth noting here is the circumstance that Marx obviously appreciates the role of the market and that of the individual in the existing mode of production. The presence of the market as the social locale of exchange and the material factuality of the individual in his/her needs and desires are obviously not doubted by Marx[37]. Indeed, their presence is assumed throughout his *oeuvre*. This is to say that Marx has always appreciated both the individuality of consumption and the social nature of planning. I would like to note this in view of the

---

435.

[37]See also MEW IV, 463; VI, 397f; VII, 19; IX, 225f; Marx's rejection of the market is directed against the attempt to describe the labor-capital-exchange as being of the same kind as the money-commodity-exchange. The latter has to be of an "analytical" kind, as he says in the "*Grundrisse*", 220, i.e. it has to be an exchange of equivalents; by this he means to say that there is nothing "synthetic" about such an exchange; it does not point beyond itself in the sense of creating value. The labor-capital-relation is, however, of a different, i.e. of a "synthetic" kind: it does point beyond itself, because it does create surplus-value, although in an exploitative way. Marx's refusal to accept that the market principle could structure the labor-capital relationship must not be confused with a rejection of the market, since the latter allows access to objects of consumption; see "*Grundrisse*", 219-231; see also MEW XVI particularly part VII "*Die Arbeitskraft*" ("The Labour Force"). It would be an entirely different question whether not even the market could disappear in a communist society, i.e. after the abolition of private property in means of production. But this is a matter of praxis not yet realized and could, therefore, only be dealt with in a speculative manner.

contemporary misunderstanding that tries to find a foundation in Marx for the idea that a whole mode of production should be either a planned economy or a market economy. This either-or-proposition has no foundation in this text or in any other portion of Marx's writings. By the same token, there is no foundation, either within or outside Marx's writings, for the claim that a capitalist economy would be exclusively controlled by "the market". There is, of course, planning at the social level in a capitalist economy, although it is hidden and is social only in distortion.

Before we turn to the next excerpt, we have to remember that Marx has so far simply indicated that he plans to bring into the open the general relations of production to distribution, exchange and consumption and that he wants to do that by taking off from the "coherence" among them. In order to make the "coherence" among all of them visible, he starts out, in the next part of this section of the "Introduction", with consumption and production, and points out that there are three identities between these two. We shall see that these identities establish a relationship between the two which has very little to do with the notion of "relation" as it prevails in Structural-Functionalism. In other words: a Structural-Functionalist approach to Marx's thought will never manage to understand his way of thinking[38]. Let us try to listen to Marx's first remarks on the first of the three identities between consumption and production:

p.90 [*Consumption and Production*]

> Production is also immediately consumption. Twofold consumption, subjective and objective: the individual not only develops his abilities in production, but also expends them, uses them up in the act of production, just as natural procreation is a consumption of life forces. Secondly: consumption of the means of production, which become worn out through use, and are partly (e.g. in combustion) dissolved into their elements again. Likewise, consumption of the raw material, which loses its natural form and

---

[38]See, in this regard also, MEW XIX, 363; EB I, 529, 539, 552.

> composition by being used up. The act of production is therefore in all its moments also an act of consumption. But the economists admit this. Production as directly identical with consumption, and consumption as directly coincident with production is termed by them *productive consumption* (Marx's italics, FWS).

In the first sentence, Marx means to say that production is consumption, in the sense that they have an "immediate" identity, i.e. one which appears to be without a mediation taking place between the two. This may not come out so clearly in the English translation, but this is the meaning in the German version, which reads "*Produktion ist unmittelbar auch Konsumtion*" which means "Production is immediately also consumption" and not "production is also immediately consumption". In the next sentence, Marx goes further by pointing out that production is consumption in a twofold sense: production is subjective and objective consumption[39]. Subjective consumption means here the consumption of the producing subject; human beings burn up their energy in production and wear themselves down. Having said that, Marx turns to the second, i.e. the objective way, in which production is consumption. In this regard, production is consumption of the means of production and of the raw material. "... production is therefore in all its moments ... consumption". "The economists admit this", and in so far Marx does not say anything new yet. He still accepts, in a way, that "production as directly identical with consumption" and vice versa, "... is termed by them (the economists, FWS) *productive consumption*" (Marx's italics).

---

[39]See the following passages in which Marx struggles with idealist, mostly Hegelian, concepts of subject and object: MEW I, 224f, 240; EB I, 227, 327; see also MEW III, 5, 218, 435. In addition let me suggest that it might not hurt to bear in mind the definitions of "subjective" and "objective" as presented in "The Concise Oxford Dictionary". There these two words are being guarded against the widespread confusion of meaning "untrue" and "true" respectively.

Together with Marx, I will return to this in a moment. Right away, though, I would like to look at a somewhat inconspicuous subclause, in which Marx surprisingly introduces a notion that, to the best of my knowledge, he has hardly ever picked up again in the particular connection with consumption and production. He says that "the individual ... develops his abilities in production". This is obviously to say that, by consuming him/her self in production, the subject experiences a growth of his/her abilities. One wonders whether Marx means to say here that learning means expending oneself and that expending oneself means learning, i.e. producing oneself. If Marx means to say that - and much speaks for it - then the latter part of my interpretation would pose problems for us today. In other words, we would have to examine those circumstances in which "expending oneself" does *not* imply learning, although Marx, differing here from us, implies, at least in my reading, that it does[40]. We, today, believe to have seen forms of production which do not develop our abilities. If what we believe to observe today is indeed the case, then we would have to investigate the reasons for this change between what happened at Marx's times and ours.

It is in the next excerpt, where Marx returns to "the economists'" concept of "productive consumption". He summarizes their point of view like this now:

> p.90 But this definition of productive consumption is advanced only for the purpose of separating consumption as identical with production from consumption proper, which is conceived rather as the destructive antithesis to production. Let us therefore examine consumption proper.

Obviously, "the economists" try to separate the consumption that takes place in the act of production from consumption proper. Marx notes that consumption "is conceived" by the economists "...as the destructive antithesis to production". He does not inspect the notion

---

[40]See also MEW III, 33; XIX, 2 (note: both passages refer to labor under communist conditions!); and also EB I, 512ff, 516, 574.

of this "destructive antithesis" further. Instead, as we shall see in the next excerpt, he treats consumption proper as consumptive production.

On "consumption proper", Marx has this to say:

> p.90 Consumption is also immediately production, just as in nature the consumption of the elements and chemical substances is the production of the plant. It is clear that in taking in food, for example, which is a form of consumption, the human being produces his own body.
> p.91 But this is also true of every kind of con-//sumption which in one way or another produces human beings in some particular aspect. Consumptive production. But, says economics, this production which is identical with consumption is secondary, it is derived from the destruction of the prior product. In the former, the producer objectified himself, in the latter, the object he created personifies itself. Hence this consumptive production - even though it is an immediate unity of production and consumption - is essentially different from production proper. The immediate unity in which production coincides with consumption and consumption with production leaves their immediate duality intact.

Marx points out that every act of consumption is a productive act as well "which in one way or another produces human beings in some particular aspect". Thus consumption is "consumptive production". Marx again, like in the inspection of "productive consumption", accepts the views of "the economists". He agrees that "this production ... is identical with consumption" and as such it "is secondary", since "it is derived from the destruction of the prior product".

For the moment, I would like to skip over the sentence (that directly follows in the above excerpt) and go straight to the point that Marx tries to make here. Since "consumptive production" is "the destruction of the prior product", it "is essentially different from production proper", even though it (consumptive production, FWS) appears as "an immediate unity of production and consumption". This unmediated unity, as it occurs, apparently without mediation between production and consumption in consumption and, as we saw above, also in production, "leaves" however, "their immediate duality intact". This is so, because production proper and consumption proper remain distinct processes. In other words, production and consumption are not just identical, but identical in distinction[41].

This result of Marx's inspection is already more than what "the economists" are saying. For him, the notion of identity is misunderstood by "the economists" as meaning simply sameness, although "the economists" try to do some "dialectical balancing of concepts" when they conceive of "consumption" as the "destructive antithesis to production". Their conceptualization of identity forgets that the identity between subject and object was already in the Idealist Theory of Knowledge (*Erkenntnistheorie*) not understood as sameness. The identity of categories between thesis and antithesis (or subject and object) was truly viewed as a dialectical relationship albeit in idealist distortion. Later towards the end of this portion on consumption and production, Marx will give primacy to production by calling it the "predominant moment". This is to say that production is the true antithesis to consumption (and also to distribution and exchange). In fact, his whole theory on labor, wage and profit is based on production as the transcending other (or the antithesis) to all other activities in the economy, in the sense of production having to generate more than what is consumed in it and in all other activities together[42].

The second aspect of the identity between consumption and production focusses on that what goes on actively between them. This aspect must also be understood in terms of its unity with, and distinction from, the first aspect. What Marx had to say about the

---

[41]Re distinction in unity see MEW VII, 20; XIX, 363; EB I, 529, 539.

[42]See e.g. the text of a talk delivered 1865 in London, published 1898 by Eleonor Aveling-Marx and Edward Aveling under the title of "Value, Price, Profit"; see MEW XVI. See also footnotes 37 and 49.

unity and duality of consumption and production served to bring out the inner correlation between the two. But there is also such a correlation between the first and the second identity. Without a distinction between the second and the first identity, and the commonality or unity between them, the second aspect had only an accidental or spurious correlation to the first one. The duality and unity between consumption and production also furnish the conditions for the possibility of a movement between the two to exist. In other words: the conditions for the duality and unity of what interacts here are the same as those for their interaction itself. In addition, the conditions for the duality in unity between consumption and production and for the interaction between the latter two have a unity as well: they are material.

This, of course, demarcates the distinction between Marx and the idealists among his predecessors with whom he has otherwise so much in common. In the debate between Kant and Leibniz, for instance, Kant gains the upper hand by proposing against Leibniz's monadology that "*relata et relatio*", i.e. what is related and the relation itself, are of a different kind. He says, e.g. about time and space as relational concepts: "*tempus et spatium sunt ordines non res*", i.e. time and space are principles of the order between things and not things themselves[43]. For Marx, however, after his critique of Hegel, relationships are as material as are the entities which they relate and from which they are, at the same time, distinct. Without the unity and duality between consumption and production and without the unity and duality between what is related and what does the

---

[43]Quoted according to Martin, op. cit., 22; see also the "*Einleitung*" there.

relating, the identity between production and consumption is incomplete[44].

Now, let us read what Marx himself has to say about this second identity:

> p.91 Production, then is also immediately consumption, consumption is also immediately production. Each is immediately its opposite. But at the same time a mediating movement takes place between the two. Production mediates consumption; it creates the latter's material; without it, consumption would lack an object. But consumption also mediates production, in that it alone creates for the products the subject for whom they are products. The product only obtains its 'last finish' in consumption. A railway on which no trains run, hence, which is not used up, not consumed, is a railway only *dynamei*, and not in reality. Without production, no consumption; but also, without consumption, no production; since production would then be purposeless.

It is perhaps interesting to note that only brief reference is being made in this quotation to the movement that "takes place between the two", i.e. between consumption and production. I think that Marx is so brief on this, because he is more interested in finding out what it is in each of them that is conditional for the actual movement of objects between them. It seems that Marx felt a greater need to elaborate on how consumption and production - regardless of their duality being contained in a unity - have yet another aspect to their

---

[44]Another aspect of a material commonality shared by distinct entities is, of course, represented by capital and wage. This is already spelt out in the first piece in which Marx concerns himself with the analysis of economic relations, namely his "*Lohnarbeit und Kapital*" ("Wage Labor and Capital") of 1849. Similar ideas emerge already before that time, e.g. in "The Second Manuscript" of the "Economic-Philosophical Manuscripts" of 1844, see MEW, EB I.

commonality. He notes that that what production does has the status of being an object for consumption. We read: "it (production, FWS) creates the latter's (consumption's, FWS) material; without it, consumption would lack an object". In other words: that what is an object for production is also an object for consumption, and that can only be, because each of the two carries in itself the related intentions or "ideals" of the other, as Marx puts it in the next excerpt.

To complete his analysis of the second identity, Marx turns matters also the other way around: "But consumption also mediates production, in that it alone creates for the products the subject for whom they are products". This means: "A railway on which no train runs, hence which is not used up, not consumed, is a railway only *dynamei*, not in reality". In other words, as a railway is consumed, i.e. worn down, it creates for the product of the railway producer a new subject, i.e. the railway makes out of itself a new subject, directly receptive for the production of new railways.

I hope that we can turn now to the third identity between production and consumption, and that we can do so by bearing in mind the two previous identities. Marx "bears them in mind" not by simply repeating them but by showing how they are transcended-and-contained in the third identity. In other words: if we want to study the third identity between these two, we have to keep in mind what Marx has to say about the ways in which both consumption and production reach into the interior aspects of one another.

We read:

p.91 Consumption produces production in a double way, (1) because a product becomes a real product only by being consumed. For example, a garment becomes a real garment only in the act of being worn; a house where no one lives is in fact not a real house; thus the product, unlike a mere natural object proves itself to be, *becomes*, a product only through consumption. Only by decomposing the product does consumption give the product the finishing touch, for the product is production not as objectified activity, but rather only as object for the active subject; (2) because consumption creates the need for *new* production, that is it creates the ideal, internally impelling cause for production, which is its presupposition. Consumption creates the motive for production; it also creates the object which is active in production as its determinant aim. If it is clear p.92 that production// offers consumption its external object, it is therefore equally clear that consumption *ideally posits* the object of production as an internal image, as a need, as drive and as purpose. It creates the objects of production in a still subjective form. No production without a need. But consumption reproduces the need.

Production, for its part, correspondingly (1) furnishes the material and the object for consumption[45]. Consumption without an object is not consumption; therefore, in this respect, production creates, produces consumption. (2) But the object is not the only thing which production creates for consumption. Production also gives consumption its specificity, its character, its finish. Just as consumption gave the product its finish as a product, so does production give finish to consumption. *Firstly*, the object is not an object in general, but a specific object which must be consumed in a specific manner, to be mediated in its turn by production itself. Hunger is hunger, but the hunger gratified by cooked meat eaten with a knife and fork is different hunger from that which bolts down raw meat with the aid of hand, nail and tooth. Production thus produces not only the object but also the manner of consumption, not only objectively but also subjectively. Production thus creates the consumer. (3) Production not only supplies a material for the need, but it also supplies a need for the material. As soon as consumption emerges from its initial state of natural crudity and immediacy - and, if it remained at that

---

[45]The English translation notes here that the manuscript says "for production", not "for consumption". This reference to the manuscript is also contained in the undated German edition of the "Introduction" that I have used for comparative purposes.

> stage, this would be because production itself had been arrested there - it becomes itself mediated as a drive by the object. The need which consumption feels for the object is created by the perception of it. The object of art - like every other product - creates a public which is sensitive to art and enjoys beauty. Production thus not only creates an object for the subject, but also a subject for the object. Thus production produces consumption (1) by creating the material for it; (2) by determining the manner of consumption; and (3) by creating the products, initially posited by it as objects, in the form of a need felt by the consumer. It thus produces the object of consumption, the manner of consumption and the motive of consumption. Consumption likewise produces the producer's *inclination* by beckoning to him as an aim-determining need (Marx's italics, FWS).

In this long excerpt, Marx inspects the various dimensions of how production and consumption give one another their specificity. He takes off from pointing out how consumption as production (first identity) allows a product to become "a real product". Then Marx relates back to an aspect of the second identity when he notes that it is in consumption that a product sees its own "finish". But then moving beyond the first and second identities, he underlines the dynamics between consumption and production: while being consumed, a product approaches the final stage of becoming what it is meant to be. Furthermore, as consumption goes on, the need for new production arises as an anticipation. Thus, consumption ideally posits the product for production as a still merely ideal image, i.e. in a subjective form. Production can only make sense, when and where there is a need for its products. This need for production is produced by consumption and it is as such proposed to production.

In the next paragraph, Marx unfolds this inner mediation further by starting out now from production. The first aspect that comes to Marx's mind is that it is production which lets consumption come about, i.e. that production creates consumption. Secondly, production gives consumption specificity by making not just any products but by making specific objects, which moreover are to be consumed in a specific way: "...the object is not an object in general, but (it is, FWS) a specific object;... to be mediated in its turn by production itself". It is in this sense, that, thirdly, production produces a specific need, not just needs in general. "The need which consumption feels for the object is created by the perception of it". "Production thus not only creates an object for the (consuming, FWS) subject, but also a subject for the object"[46]. These three aspects of the third identity between consumption and production are summarized this way. "It (production, FWS) thus produces the object of consumption, the manner of consumption and motive of consumption".

In the very last sentence of this excerpt, Marx returns to a consideration he has dealt with before in this excerpt, namely to the circumstance that "... consumption reproduces the need". Now he carries that thought further by elaborating on how consumption produces an inclination inside the producer to be what he is, namely a producer of specific goods, not a producer in general. The producer comes to notice in himself the specificity of the consumer's need "by (the consumer, FWS) beckoning (the inclination, FWS) to him (the producer, FWS) as an aim-determining need". In other words, this beckoning turns the consumer's need into an "aim-determining need" for the producer.

After having followed Marx's analysis of the three identities between consumption and production, we hopefully see not only the duality and unity, or distinction in identity, of the two and the directedness that they have towards one another, but we also see how the innermost nature of each of the two is in the other in such a way that we know why they belong together. They do not just stand in "a relationship" with one another, as Structural Functionalists would

---

[46]The creation of a subject for consumption has, of course, become a professional activity today: advertisements. I am not aware of Marx having dealt with that kind of unproductive labor extensively somewhere else. In Late Capitalism, advertising has become a necessary unproductive labor. Without it, the present consumerism and its implicit high level of productivity would be unthinkable.

say, we now can understand why they have a being that is intrinsically a being for one another.

Before Marx turns to the identity between distribution and production, he tries to fend off a typically idealist misunderstanding of "identity", in this case still that of production and consumption. In doing so, he makes explicit reference to the notion of production being the "predominant moment" in the relation between consumption and production. This allows us to get a better feel for Marx's concept of the material dialectic between consumption and production. Let's read the text first:

> p.93 Thereupon, nothing simpler for a Hegelian than to posit production and consumption as identical. And this has been done not only by socialist belletrists but by prosaic p.94 economists them//selves, e.g. Say; in the form that when one looks at an entire people, its production is its consumption. Or, indeed, at humanity in the abstract. Storch demonstrated Say's error, namely that e.g. a people does not consume its entire product, but also creates means of production, etc., fixed capital, etc. To regard society as one single subject is, in addition, to look at it wrongly; speculatively. With a single subject, production and consumption appear as moments of a single act. The important thing to emphasize here is only that, whether production and consumption are viewed as the activity of one or of many individuals, they appear in any case as moments of one process, in which production is the real point of departure and hence also the predominant moment. Consumption as urgency, as need, is itself an intrinsic moment of productive activity. But the latter is the point of departure for realization and hence also its predominant moment; it is the act through which the whole process again runs its course. The individual produces an object and, by consuming it, returns to himself, but returns as a productive and self-reproducing individual. Consumption thus appears as a moment of production.

> In society, however, the producer's relation to the product, once the latter is finished, is an external one, and its return to the subject depends on his relations to other individuals. He does not come into possession of it directly. Nor is its immediate appropriation his purpose when he produces in society. *Distribution* steps between the producers and the products, hence between production and consumption, to determine in accordance with social laws what the producer's share will be in the world of products.
> Now, does distribution stand at the side of and outside production as an autonomous sphere? (Marx's italics, FWS).

It may come to some of us as a surprise that Marx lumps together "a Hegelian", "socialist belletrists"[47] and "prosaic economists"[48]. He does so, other commonalities among them notwithstanding, because they all "posit production and consumption as identical". One of them, namely Jean-Baptiste Say (who had simplified Adam Smith's Political Economy into some sort of a textbook) had done that in saying that when one looks at an entire people, its production is its consumption.

In his critique of this kind of a position, Marx takes off from the circumstance that Heinrich-Friedrich Storch (at that time a professor of Political Economy in St. Petersburg) had already "demonstrated Say's error", by showing that one could see, even when looking at a society as a whole, more than an identity in the sense of sameness

---

[47]He does so frequently in "The Holy Family" (MEW II, 3-223), "The German Ideology" (MEW III, 9-530) and "The Misery of Philosophy" (MEW IV, 63-182). Very often, Marx understands by "socialist belletrists" in particular French writers like St. Simon, Comte, Say, Bastiat and Proudhon. See also MEW XVII, 643.

[48]Marx subsumes under this label Political Economists, among them most prominently Adam Smith and David Ricardo, but also other writers like Alfred Darimont, Edward Wakefield, Jean-Charles de Sismondis and John Stuart Mill, to name but a few.

between production and consumption. A society always produces more than it consumes, since "...a people does not consume its entire product, but also creates means of production, etc. fixed capital, etc."[49]. This already is a good reason to see that production is "predominant". But Marx also notes that "... in addition...(T)o regard society as one single subject is...to look at it wrongly; speculatively". In other words, there are two mistakes being made here by Say (and the likes): 1.- To say that production equals consumption misses the synthetic nature of their relationship. 2.- To see the entire society as one whole (or as a unit) is to see it "wrongly" and "speculatively".

Indicatively, Marx treats these mistakes concurrently. However, he does not deal directly with the first mistake, because he obviously thinks that Storch had taken care of that. His treatment of the second mistake transcends-and-contains not only Storch's remarks on the first mistake, but also teaches the "Hegelians" a lesson that is already waiting to be pointed out within Storch's words. Unfolding this will, hopefully, allow us to understand why Marx calls the position of his idealist opponents "wrong" and "speculative".

After its initial adoption, Marx drops his opponents' position as irrelevant and he does so vis-a-vis aspects intrinsic to production and consumption at the materially concrete level. This is to say that, while trying a true critique delivered from within his opponents' position, he goes straight to the heart of things at hand, which comes into sight regardless of what position it is that determines, as a mental construct, an observer's subjective view. He says: "the important thing to emphasize here is only that, whether production and consumption are viewed as the activity of one or of many individuals, they appear in any case as moments of one process, in which

---

[49]Marx thinks here of production as the creation of surplus value. To the extent that its appropriation by the capitalist (and the disastrous consequences of this) is Marx's main concern since he turned his attention to the study of Political Economy - see footnotes 24, 37, 44 - references to passages where he emphasizes the "predominant" status of production have to be severely limited here. I think that one of the passages that lends access to the concept of surplus value most easily can be found in "*Grundrisse*", 219-231.

production is the real point of departure and hence also the predominant moment". Marx backs this up by summarizing what he has said earlier about the identity between production and consumption.

In the last two sentences of the first paragraph of this excerpt Marx adds further clarification to the notion of production being the "predominant moment". He does that in a way which goes even beyond the level of production creating surplus as Storch had pointed out already. This surplus production has not only to be there, when one looks at a singularly producing subject, be that an individual or "a people", since even then "(T)he individual...by consuming it (the product, FWS)...returns as a productive and self-reproducing individual" to himself. It is intrinsically this which makes "consumption...a moment of production", and, therefore gives one an additional reason to see production as the "predominant moment" between "production" and "consumption".

At this point, however, one begins to wonder whether the word "predominant" is not a poor translation of the German "*das Übergreifende*". "*Das Übergreifende*" certainly implies that production is the commonality between production and consumption (as described above). It also indicates that production is in a sense more than consumption; it transcends consumption. It goes insofar beyond the level of surplus creation as it is more important that production takes place in consumption than consumption in production. The wear-and-tear that takes place in production needs to be compensated by re-producing the productive means including human beings through consumption. This way consumption becomes visible as a mere moment of production. Storch's correct reference to the production of surplus as an indication of the "predominance" of production is now transcended-and-contained in a richer understanding of the distinction in the unity between production and consumption.

I hope that we are now in a position to understand better what Marx means, when he calls the approach of those whom he critiques as "wrong" and "speculative". In this regard it is important to note first that Marx takes off from what materially goes on in production and consumption, i.e. he does not come to the inspection of these two "speculatively". By grounding himself in the materially concrete, he appreciates that the identity between production and consumption is a synthetic one which one would notice even when treating society "in the abstract" as a unit (which it materially is not). By taking off from the materially concrete as a productive synthesis, he can avoid making statements that originate in a "posited" position. "(t)o posit production and consumption as identical" (and not as synthetic) is a mental construct that "a Hegelian", "socialist belletrists" and "prosaic economists" have in common. As such, their statements would still be, like all statements, of a synthetic kind themselves - Marx would not deny them that status - except that these statements are idealist syntheses between the observers' mind set (categories) and the reality out there. Statements of this kind are, "wrong" and "speculative". As idealist statements they synthesize a merely mental subjectivity with the world out there and thus miss the world, because the idealist relationship to the world has no sense for the material nature of the duality and unity between the human being and the world. In other words, Marx makes reference here to the obvious circumstance that a sense for the primacy of the materially concrete is missing in these statements. Since "a Hegelian", "socialist belletrists" and "prosaic economists" act as if economic life "had made its way ... from the textbooks into reality", as Marx has reason to remark a little earlier in his "Introduction" (p. 90), they fail to learn from the world of things by persisting in making merely mental projections into that world. That is to say that these opponents of his have to engage in "the task ..." of "... the dialectic balancing of concepts and not the grasping of real relations"[50].

---

[50]Besides the circumstance that objections against idealist projections into the world "out there" have been the focus of those of Marx's writings that accompany or follow soon after his"Theses on Feuerbach", namely "The Holy Family" and "The German Ideology", the following passages also expressing these objections may be of interest here: MEW I, 203 passim and especially the remarks on Hegel 305ff, 378f; IV, 134f; XIX, 403f; XXXII, 547; see also EB I, 294.

Marx knows, of course, of the synthetic nature of all, including his own, statements. However, the issue is to retain awareness, in the present connection, for the circumstance that production and consumption are synthetic in themselves, even if no observing subject, be they "a Hegelian", "socialist belletrists", "prosaic economists" (or dialectical materialists!) were around. For the observer, the issue arises whether his (synthetic) statements about this kind of a material synthesis in fact transcend-and-contain that material synthesis conceptually. Marx does obviously not doubt that such kind of an adequate transcendence can be achieved. This certainty, possibly surprising for most of us today, allows him the security of his judgement about his opponents, as being "wrong" and "speculative". This certainty is grounded in the sensuality of his "Method of Political Economy" to which he devotes a whole section of the "Introduction". Although we have to concern ourselves with that section a little later, it may be appropriate, given the present context, to point out that that section could be considered a "Treatise on Learning", not the least because it advocates so strongly to ground all understanding primarily in the concrete. In this sense, the present rejection of "a Hegelian", "socialist belletrists" and "prosaic economists" receives further elaboration in that section on "Method", particularly in those portions of it that deal with the "theoretical appropriation of the world".

Marx ends his inspection of consumption and production by pointing out that "... in society, ... the subject... does not come into possession of it (the product, FWS) directly ... *Distribution* (Marx's italics) steps between ... production and consumption". Given this position of distribution, Marx's central question in this connection is: "...does distribution stand at the side of and outside production as an autonomous sphere?". As an entry into his treatment of this question the following excerpt may be helpful:

p.96 In the shallowest conception, distribution appears as the distribution of products, and hence as further removed from and quasi-independent of production. But before distribution can be the distribution of products, it is: (1) the distribution of the instruments of production, and (2), which is a further specification of the same relation, the distribution of the members of the society among the different kinds of production. (Subsumption of the individuals under specific relations of production.) The distribution of products is evidently only a result of this distribution, which is comprised within the process of production itself and determines the structure of production.

While I think that this characterization of distribution speaks largely for itself, I would nevertheless like to underline that Marx studies distribution, as he has done with production and consumption, in its materially concrete occurrence, namely when it is enacted in (not just planned for) the activities of production. For him, "...distribution... is comprised within the process of production itself". As such distribution is "(1) the distribution of the instruments of production" and "(2) the distribution of the members of the society among the different kinds of production". The concrete enactment of distribution within production comes "before distribution can be the distribution of products". This is obviously stated in anticipation of his treatment of exchange, as the latter makes products accessible to consumption. This implies the immanence of distribution in all other aspects of the economy. Ignoring this has had surprising consequences for the understanding of distribution on the part of some political economists. Marx notes:

p.94 When one examines the usual works of economics, it is immediately striking that everything in them is posited
p.95 doubly.// For example, ground rent, wages, interest and profit figure under distribution, while land, labour and capital figure under production as agents of production. In the case of capital, now, it is evident from the outset that it is posited doubly, (1) as agent of production, (2) a source of income, as a determinant of specific forms of distribution.

and, also on

p.95 The category ("*Rubrik*", in German, FWS) of wages, similarly, is the same as that which is examined under a

> different heading as wage labour: the characteristic which labour here possesses as an agent of production appears as a characteristic of distribution. If labour were not specified as wage labour, then the manner in which it shares in the products would not appear as wages; as, for example, under slavery.

The first sentence of these two excerpts obviously strikes a more general theme, one that relates to a widespread feature of works in economics. Although the tone of that sentence is undoubtedly announcing a rejection of what "usual works of economics" have to say, Marx, as a true critic, still takes off from their position. And yet, as we shall see, he does not only bear in mind that, when "everything ... (is) posited doubly", this "rupture had made its way ... from reality into the textbooks ..." (p. 90 of the "Introduction"), but also that this rupture indicates two other important aspects: He points out that this "double positing", on the one hand, indicates the duality between distribution and production, and, on the other, shows, later on in connection with Ricardo, how little these "usual works of economics" are capable of seeing the unity in that duality. Of course, if one thinks only in terms of segregating definitions, then one has a hard time to see an inner unity, a mediation between such mentally segregated entities. Needless to say, labor and wage, just to select one of the pairs involved here, are not the same, but they represent an identity. It is their identity in the distinction of a duality which allows them to enter into a relationship to one another as parts of a concrete economic process. "If labour were not specified as wage labour, then ... it ... would not appear as wages; as, for example, under slavery"[51].

While the identity between distribution and production does not simply imply their sameness, their duality does not segregate them either; they do not stand outside one another, as "works of economics" assume. Ricardo, for instance, treats the two this way and thus gets into considerable conceptual problems. Marx writes:

---

[51]See also MEW II, 37; XIX, 2; EB I, 473f, 529.

> p.96 To examine production while disregarding this internal distribution within it is obviously an empty abstraction; while conversely, the distribution of products follows by itself from this distribution which forms an original moment of production. Ricardo, whose concern was to grasp the specific social structure of modern production,
> p.97 and who//is the economist of production *par excellence*, declares for precisely that reason that *not* production but distribution is the proper study of modern economics. This again shows the ineptitude of those economists who portray production as an eternal truth while banishing history to the realm of distribution (Marx's italics, FWS).

In this excerpt, Marx means to say that one would study "an empty abstraction"[52] were one to examine production while ignoring the "internal distribution within it". This, however, is exactly what Ricardo is doing. As a consequence, he has to make distribution the "proper study of economics", although his "concern was ... modern production". Production on its part is turned into something a-historical, always obeying "inviolable natural laws"[53] as Marx put it above (p. 87 of the "Introduction"), while in "distribution ... humanity has allegedly permitted itself to be considerably more arbitrary" (ibid.). Not seeing the unity in the duality of production and distribution "... shows the ineptitude of those economists who portray production as an eternal truth while banishing history to the realm of distribution". Seeing the relationship between distribution and production this way as being only an external one is a logical consequence of accepting a "rupture" in what really forms a totality.

And yet, let us bear in mind that the totality formed by distribution and production out there in the reality of the praxis is not even seen by those directly involved in that praxis. The "rupture" exists out there and "has made its way ... into the textbooks". Is this not to say that the theoretical mind of the political economist cannot

---

[52]See in this regard MEW II, 60-62.

[53]MEW II, 135f; III, 43ff; EB I, 515f, 536, 543f, 587.

even trust what the practitioners of reality tell him? Surely, for the latter, labor and wage are a distinct duality and their unity is not appreciated; they posit the two "doubly" as well. This implies, as we shall see in our reading of Section Two of the "Introduction", that the "Method of Political Economy" has nothing else to take off from than the materially concrete and, in doing so, has to understand critically how the materially concrete is conceptualized by those involved in its enactment and then also by those theorizing about it.

In the following excerpt, Marx tries to show that distribution and production change together, i.e. they do so in unity. This allows for the conceptualization of production in terms of the primacy that it has at the materially concrete level anyways. Here, Marx goes back to a thought that he had already expressed in his study of consumption and production. We read:

p. 97 The question of the relation between this production-determining distribution, and production, belongs evidently within production itself. If it is said that, since production must begin with a certain distribution of the instruments of production, it follows that distribution at least in this sense precedes and forms the presupposition of production, then the reply must be that production does indeed have its determinants and preconditions, which form its moments. At the very beginning these may appear as spontaneous, natural. But by the process of production itself they are transformed from natural into historic determinants, and if they appear to one epoch as natural presuppositions of production, they were its historic product for another. Within production itself they are constantly being changed. The application of machinery, for example, changed the distribution of instruments of production as well as of products. Modern large-scale landed property is itself the product of modern commerce and of modern industry as well as of the application of the latter to agriculture.

Certainly, distribution appears in its form in production and, as Marx says on p. 96 of the "Introduction" (not excerpted here), "to the single individual, ... distribution appears as a social law which determines his position within the system of production..., and which therefore precedes production", but it is production which generates everything that can be consumed, exchanged and distributed. It does so by generating more than is being consumed and is required for doing the work of distribution and exchange. Therefore, production is the agent of growth and change. "Within production itself", so we read in the above excerpt, "they (the determinants of production, FWS) are constantly being changed". For this reason, production is the "predominant moment" as we read on p. 94 of the "Introduction", i.e. it transcends-and-contains the other aspects of the economic process. Logical primacy belongs to production and not to distribution, although the latter may appear to be "predominant to the individual" or to the economist who have uncritically accepted the "rupture" among the parts which form the socio-economic totality.

Towards the end of this whole section on "Distribution and Production", Marx turns briefly to the question of whether the law[54] can perpetuate forms of distribution. He indicates that he does not think that property laws (i.e. formal regulations that govern distribution) can do much to keep production from pressing forward and changing the distribution of ownership:

p.98 Laws may perpetuate an instrument of production, e.g. land, in certain families. These laws achieve economic significance only when large-scale landed property is in harmony with the society's production, as e.g. in England. In France, small-scale agriculture survived despite the great landed estates, hence the latter were smashed by the revolution. But can laws perpetuate the small-scale allotment? Despite these laws, ownership is again becoming concentrated. The influence of laws in

---

[54]Regarding the law, see e.g. MEW I, 273, 364f; III, 62ff, 311ff; VI, 244ff; XIX, 20f.

> stabilizing relations of distribution, and hence their effect on production, requires to be determined in each specific instance.

As Marx points out here, the small scale landownership legally introduced in France during the French Revolution led later again to growing concentration; capital interests demanded that. This is to show again that production is the driving force in economics and not distribution.

I would also like to think that Marx has by now answered the question with which he entered his inspection of the relationship between production and distribution namely: "Does distribution stand at the side and outside production as an autonomous sphere?". He does answer that question in two ways: 1.- Distribution and production mediate one another. Distribution is enacted in production and distribution is a productive activity. That is to say that the two are a unity in duality. For this reason alone, it is already totally inadequate to think of the two first as standing "at the side" of one another and then as being somehow related to one another. 2.- Their relationship is not only grounded in their mediation, one of the two, namely production, has also to be conceptualized as the "predominant" aspect, not only because it is the surplus generating and thus the driving force between these two as well as among all other aspects of economics, but also because all other aspects of the economy are "mere moments of production".

While Marx leaves a further consideration of legal matters to "each specific instance", it needs to be noted that he ventures, on a number of occasions in this section on "Distribution and Production", beyond any "specific instance", even beyond the realm of Capitalism. It can not be denied that he draws upon examples from the Turks and Romans, the Mongols and the Germanic Barbarians, in order to make his point on distribution. It is references like these which have suggested to people that Marx claims universal applicability to his critique of the political economy of Capitalism. This obviously contradicts an assertion to the opposite that I made above. In view of this I would like to point out that the "*Grundrisse*" was written in the winter of 1857/8 and the "Introduction" even a few weeks before that. At that time, it may very well not have come to Marx's full attention that a "superhistorical theory" on history was an impossible undertaking, a contradiction-in-itself. This insight, clearly spelt out 20 years later in his life, was nevertheless already germinating in his thinking. An important seedbed for the germination of this can be found in his contemplations on "Method".

Before Marx takes us into these contemplations, he spends just a little more than one page on "Exchange and Production". The latter half of that section does not even place exchange anymore into the center of its concern. It is used to present a summary of this whole second portion of the "Introduction", as it is dedicated to "The General Relation of Production to Distribution, Exchange, Consumption". And yet, what is being said there on exchange allows one to clarify two additional aspects intrinsic to this "General Relation". Let us first read the following excerpt:

> p.99 In so far as *exchange* is merely a moment mediating between production with its production-determined distribution on one side and consumption on the other, but in so far as the latter itself appears as a moment of production, to that extent is exchange obviously also included as a moment within the latter.
>
> It is clear, firstly, that the exchange of activities and abilities which takes place within production itself belongs directly to production and essentially constitutes it. The same holds, secondly, for the exchange of products, in so far as that exchange is the means of finishing the product and making it fit for direct consumption. To that extent, exchange is an act comprised within production itself. Thirdly, the so-called exchange between dealers and dealers is by its very organization entirely determined by production, as well as being itself a producing activity (Marx's italics, FWS).

In the first paragraph of this excerpt, Marx indicates that exchange is not just "a moment mediating between production...

distribution... and consumption", but that it also is "included as a moment within production". He then unfolds that includedness under the first two points of the next paragraph. This shows again how the one is internal to the other, explaining this way again not only *that* but also *why* these parts of an economic system can relate to one another.

As a third aspect, Marx speaks about the "exchange between dealers and dealers". He does not only see it as "entirely determined by production", he also sees exchange "as being itself a producing activity", i.e. having an identity in distinction with it. In as much as consumption "finishes" production, dealerships which mediate between producer and consumer help in this "finishing" process. This needs to be borne in mind as only a product actually put at the disposal of productive consumption by a dealer can get its "finish". Being part of the productive activities of society does not mean that exchange adds any value to the product. It only means that labor still necessary for the finishing of production is performed in exchange. This way, production reaches into exchange, takes place in it, without becoming the same as exchange.

The last paragraph of this second section of the "Introduction" reads:

p.99 The conclusion we reach is not that production, distribution, exchange and consumption are identical, but they all form the members of a totality, distinctions within a unity. Production predominates not only over itself, in the antithetical definition of production, but over the other moments as well. The process always returns to production to begin anew. That exchange and consumption cannot be predominant is self-evident. Likewise, distribution as distribution of products; while as distribution of the agents of production it is itself a moment of production. A definite production thus determines a definite consumption, distribution and exchange as well as *definite relations between these different moments*. Admittedly, however, *in its one-sided form*, production is itself determined by the

> other moments. For example if the market, i.e. the sphere of exchange, expands, then production grows in quantity and the divisions between its different branches become deeper.
>
> p.100 A change in distribution//changes production, e.g. concentration of capital, different distribution of the population between town and country, etc. Finally, the needs of consumption determine production. Mutual interaction takes place between the different moments. This the case with every organic whole (Marx's italics, FWS).

This paragraph takes the reader quite abruptly out of the treatment of "Exchange and Production" into a summary of the whole of Part Two of the "Introduction" without providing a new title. Given that Part Two is quite long and deals with a rather difficult topic, half a page of a summary would appear to be a pretty short treatment. And yet, provided the reader has carefully studied Part Two, this summary gives him an opportunity to check whether he has fully understood a set of concepts that is quite fundamental for Marx's thought.

The first sentence of this summary rejects a notion prevailing among his opponents, i.e. the "Hegelians", the "socialist belletrists" and the "prosaic economists". Marx states that it is not "(T)he conclusion we reach ... that production, distribution, exchange and consumption are identical...", i.e. they are not the same. Instead, they have an identity among them. That is to say that each is materially contained in the other three and all are in each of them. "...they all form the members of a totality", because each shares that totality[55] not by making each of them uniform, but by giving each "distinctions within a unity". The commonality among them does not just allow for the existence of relations among them that are external to each of them, but for external relations that are grounded in internal properties shared by each of them.

---

[55]Regarding the notion of the totality being contained in its parts, see: MEW IV, 130; XIX, 363; EB I, 538f.

Then Marx turns his attention to production by immediately reminding us of production "in its antithetical definition". Obviously, he does not want to fall into the danger of treating production "in its one-sided form". In other words, Marx repeats that production is not only contained in all the other aspects of the economy, but it also transcends them and therefore "determines a definite consumption, distribution and exchange". In addition, he says again that without production generating what goes beyond all these others, i.e. without a surplus generating production, consumption, distribution and exchange could not be and could not occur in the specific form in which they do take place.

The "predominance" of production is, however, not turning it into the sole agent of expansion, i.e. of economic growth, because production, even "in its one-sided form ..." i.e. in itself "... is determined by the other moments". Surplus as a transcending aspect of production can only realize itself in growth, if it receives determination from the others. If, "(F)or example, ... the market, i.e. the sphere of exchange, expands, production (and thus capital, FWS) grows in quantity" too.

Having arrived at the end of Part Two of the "Introduction", I think that all these observations allow us to understand Marx's concept of "the general" better. First of all, "the general" means an intrinsic commonality among distinct entities in a specific and materially concrete way. "The general" is not an a-historically postulated concept of the general so much searched for by thinkers of Marx's time (and today). Instead Marx speaks of a generality that is specific for a determinate set of entities and their relations.

Secondly, "the general" identifies a totality that is within each of its parts. In this regard, Marx clearly stands in the Kantian-Hegelian tradition. As I have said above (p. 3), with an eye on Kant for instance, the twelve categories "are not only a consistent part of Newton's knowledge ... they also contain the totality of it...". Marx, however, gives that philosophical insight a materialist, dynamic and, for that matter, a dialectic dimension. He speaks of materially occurring interactions, namely the ones in the economy, and he sees, contrary to the historically stagnant concept of synthesis a la Kant and also ultimately a la Hegel, a dynamic synthesis in the material processes between production, consumption and so forth. At the same time, however, he does not speak of production as the sole agent of synthesis in the same way as Kant and Hegel have spoken of the human subject or more precisely speaking, of the mind of the subject, as the lonesome spiritual agent of understanding and history. Marx, instead, emphasizes that the dynamics of history, as they originate in production, can only take place in "... the mutual interaction... between the different moments" of the economic process. This is why Marx speaks of "The General Relations of Production *to* Distribution, Exchange, Consumption" and not of the general relation *among* production, distribution, exchange and consumption (italics added, FWS). He wishes to express, even in the title of this section, that production is one among others of a totality, but is as such the "predominant", or better, the transcending one.

There is, furthermore, a remark in this summary which brings back an aspect in the relations among the various moments of production that Marx has referred to before and which helps us on our way into Part Three of the "Introduction".

In the above excerpt, Marx writes that "when production grows in quantity", then "the divisions between its different branches become deeper". Earlier in his text, that is on p. 90 in the last sentence of his opening remarks on "The General Relation...", Marx has spoken about the same "divisions between the different branches" in terms of a "rupture" among them. That sentence reads: "As if this rupture had made its way not from reality into the textbooks, but rather from the textbooks into reality, and as if the task were the dialectic balancing of concepts, and not the grasping of real relations". As the reader may be aware, I have quoted that sentence twice already above (p. 37 and p. 55), but I did so by placing emphasis separately on the two "wrongs" which Marx, however, addresses in unity, as it were. He sees that committing the mistake of treating the "rupture" as having come into reality from the textbooks as implying the next mistake, namely that of seeing "the dialectic balancing of concepts" instead of "the grasping of real relations" as one's task.

It would appear to be obvious that Marx means to say that the task of the student of economics is to *not* engage in "the dialectic balancing of concepts", but in "the grasping of real relations". But does the rejection of this task mean that Marx accepts the "rupture" between production, distribution, exchange and consumption, as it has come "from reality into the textbooks"? Certainly not! He has, at no point in his treatment of "the general relation of production" to "the other branches", accepted the "barbarically tearing apart (of) things which belong together" (p. 89 of the "Introduction"), although he acknowledges here, as he does throughout the text, that the economic praxis has developed in a way so that "the divisions between the different parts (of the economy, FWS) became deeper". However deep this rupture may have become, Marx has brought into the open that among the various aspects of the economy, there is still a "unity", a "commonality", a "mediation" without which they could not do what they in fact do, namely stand in relations to one another. They *do* that *materially*, regardless of what the practitioners and theoreticians say about them[56]. The problem of most of the writers on Political Economy is that they have mentally fallen prey to a praxis that tears apart in its own self-understanding what in material reality still is a totality, namely the totality of production, distribution, exchange and consumption. This indicates that it is the issue in an attempt to understand the materially concrete, not to let that, which is merely an appearance of the materially concrete for those practising it, enter into the books, nor to project, as an observer, one's own literature derived ideas into reality, but to move, reflexively and critically, from the materially concrete in its totality to the abstractions as they are practically at work in the concrete.

The question of how Marx proposes to do that is dealt with in Part Three of the "Introduction", namely the section on "The Method of Political Economy", to which we now turn.

---

[56]It should be clear that Marx who knows so much about the false consciousness of people does not propose that a researcher while doing social research should simply accept what people say about themselves. See among many other passages, MEW VIII, 139f. See also pp.20f above.

3.- Marx's Method: The Dynamics of Coming to Know

Let us first pay attention to an excerpt taken from the almost two page long second paragraph of "The Method":

p.100 It seems to be correct to begin with the real and the concrete, with the real precondition, thus to begin, in economics, with e.g. the population, which is the foundation and the subject of the entire social act of production. However, on closer examination this proves false. The population is an abstraction if I leave out for example, the classes of which it is composed. These classes in turn are an empty phrase if I am not familiar with the elements on which they rest. E.g. wage labour, capital, etc. These latter in turn presuppose exchange, division of labour, prices, etc. For example, capital is nothing without wage labour, without value, money, price etc. Thus, if I were to begin with the population, this would be a chaotic conception [*Vorstellung*] of the whole, and I would then, by means of further determination, move analytically towards ever more simple concepts [*Begriff*], from the imagined concrete towards ever thinner abstractions until I had arrived at the simplest determinations. From there the journey would have to be retraced until I had finally arrived at the population again, but this time not as the chaotic conception of a whole, but as a rich totality of many determinations and relations. The former is the path historically followed by economics at the time of its origins. The economists of the seventeenth century, e.g., always begin with the living whole, with population, nation, state, several states, etc.; but they always conclude by discovering through analysis a small number of determinant, abstract, general relations such as division of labour, money, value, etc. As soon as these individual moments had been more or less firmly established and abstracted, there began the economic systems, which ascended from the simple relations, p. 101 such as labour, division of labour, need, //exchange value, to the level of the state, exchange between nations and the world market. The latter is obviously the scientifically correct method. The concrete is concrete because it is the concentration of many determinations, hence unity of the diverse. It appears in the process of thinking, therefore, as a process of concentration, as a result, not as a point of departure, even though it is the point of departure in reality and hence also the point of departure for observation [*Anschauung*] and conception. Along the first path the full conception was evaporated to yield an abstract determination; along the second, the abstract determinations lead towards a reproduction of the concrete by way of thought. In this way Hegel fell into the illusion of conceiving the real as the product of thought concentrating itself, probing its own depths, and unfolding itself out of itself, by itself, whereas the method of rising from the abstract to the concrete is only the way in which thought appropriates the concrete, reproduces it as the concrete in the mind. But this is by no means the process by which the concrete itself comes into being. For example, the simplest economic category, say e.g. exchange value, presupposes population, moreover a population producing in specific relations; as well as a certain kind of family, or commune, or state, etc. It can never exist other than as an abstract, one-sided relation within an already given, concrete, living whole. As a category, by contrast, exchange value leads an antediluvian existence. Therefore, to the kind of consciousness - and this is characteristic of the philosophical

> consciousness - for which conceptual thinking is the real human being, and for which the conceptual world as such is thus the only reality, the movement of the categories appears as the real act of production - which only, unfortunately, receives a jolt from the outside - whose product is the world; and - but this is again a tautology - this is correct in so far as the concrete totality is a totality of thoughts, concrete in thought, in fact a product of thinking and comprehending; but not in any way a product of the concept which thinks and generates itself outside or above observation and conception; a product, rather, of the working-up of observation and conception into concepts. The totality as it appears in the head, as a totality of thoughts, is a product of a thinking head, which appropriates the world in the only way it can, a way different from the artistic, religious, practical and mental appropriation of this world. The real subject retains its autonomous existence outside the head just as before; namely as long as// the head's conduct is merely speculative, merely theoretical. Hence, in the theoretical method, too, the subject, society, must always be kept in mind as the presupposition (bracketed italics added by the translator, FWS).

p.102

I do not think that too many readers will have difficulties with the first sentence in this excerpt, in which Marx calls the "population" the "real" and "concrete" precondition and foundation for the entire social act of production. For this reason, though, it will be all the more puzzling to many of us when he suggests in the next sentence, that "this proves false", i.e. to begin with the population in an attempt to study "a given country politico - economically" as he puts it occasionally (see e.g. p. 100 of the "Introduction", in a paragraph not excerpted here). Marx tells us that the reason for his judgement is that "the population is an abstraction". In other words, what appears to be something real and concrete is seen by Marx as an abstraction.[57]

Leaving aside, for the moment, Marx's reasoning about his judgement, one should remember that he, in his attempts to come to grips with the meaning of the reality of his time, had to do battle on two fronts. He did not only oppose the Idealism of the Hegelians but also the stifling propositions of Positivism, as they came from the "socialist belletrists". His objection against the latter and their simplistic acceptance of the concrete is a direct rejection of ideas that had been subsumed, e.g. by St. Simon and Comte, under terms like "self-evidence" or "sense-evidence". Marx knew that the meaning of phenomena is only under special circumstances (to be inspected later, namely pp. 97ff) directly accessible to our senses. Or, in other words, as long as we do not know the constitutive aspects of phenomena, of which Marx otherwise speaks as their determinations and their commonalities, these phenomena remain abstractions for the theoretical mind, no matter how real and concrete they may appear to our senses.

It is for this reason that Marx proceeds cautiously in the next few lines of the above excerpt in his attempt to turn what we might call the abstractly concrete into a concrete abstraction. On this occasion, we have an opportunity to witness how he moves, like an archaeologist, deeper and deeper, layer by layer, into the constitutive aspects of what, in this case, "population" means "in a given country". The aspects that Marx comes to inspect at the various layers as being constitutive to the "conception" of "population" are "classes", then "wage labour" and "capital", and finally "money" and "price". Marx, reflecting on his archaeology, notes: "Thus, if I were to begin with population..." as it is directly accessible to our sense-evidence, I would begin with "a chaotic conception", or, as he says a little later, with an "imagined concrete". This means that the visibly evident is a chaotic imagination as long as its determinations

---

[57]Regarding this view see also MEW I, 233ff, 313; II, 38, 60ff; EB I, 294.

and the relations among them have not been unearthed[58]. The process of this archaeology, "move(s), analytically towards ever more simple concepts".

The characterization of these elements as "simple" or even "simplest determinations" on the one hand, and as "ever thinner abstractions", on the other, obviously indicates that Marx equates the simplest with the thinnest abstractions. While this was a use of terms quite common, at least in the writings of Kant and some others since then (and still very much so in Mathematics today), the meaning of these terms may require a bit of an explanation today. Let us remember, for a moment, that Kant had analyzed Newton's mechanics with regard to its ultimate, i.e. simplest constitutive concepts. The twelve categories which Kant uncovered in this process, could not be divided any further into constitutive aspects. As concepts, these categories were highly abstract, i.e. not concrete or open to direct sensual evidence. As the "simplest determinations" they were the "thinnest abstractions".

While this may help to make Marx's use of these terms a little bit more plausible to us, we should not ignore that Marx has only spoken so far about half of the task involved in a process of understanding. Marx suggests now, i.e. after having arrived at those "thinnest abstractions", that "... the journey would have to be retraced until I had finally arrived at the population again, but this time not as the chaotic conception of a whole, but as a rich totality of many determinations and relations". Then the abstractly concrete, namely the concept of "population", has become a concrete abstraction, i.e. its intangible and nonvisible meaning has become concrete for us; we know it.

---

[58]Prior to such archaeology, understanding is for Marx, of course, suffering from false consciousness; see MEW III, 233; also take note of I, 240f; III, 113f, IV, 130; EB I, 297, 539. The potentially ubiquitous presence of false consciousness implies that the form and meaning of a social object are not directly visible either; see, regarding the difference between "class" and "estate" for instance, MEW III, 62.

Marx of whom we heard before that he is opposed to the projection of textbook ideas into the study of the economic process makes it the first point in his "Method of Political Economy" to suggest that it is "...correct to begin (in one's study, FWS) with the real and the concrete". But this suggestion, so we understand now, does not imply an advocacy of "sense-evidence" in the positivist sense. Marx knows that the meaning of the concrete is not obvious, but is an abstraction. Therefore, while the obvious and the concrete have to be the departure point for getting at the meaning of the concrete, the concrete and the evidently given cannot be more than a departure point. The process of coming to know is a two-way journey; it is first the attempt at unearthing, layer by layer, the meaning that phenomena have "in a given society", and then the return from that abstraction to the concrete aspects of the phenomena under consideration.

In the next three or four sentences, Marx makes reference to the ways in which the economists of the seventeenth century went about their business of analyzing a society "politico-economically". He reminds the reader that these scholars also went back to the most simple, or, as he puts it, to the "individual moments" of an economic system, after having started out at the level of the "living whole". Then similar to Marx's own proposal, they returned from these "simple relations" again "to the level of the state" and even to "the world market". This way of analyzing "a given country ... is obviously the scientifically correct method".

Having characterized the approach of these earlier economists as not yet suffering from a positivist acceptance of sense-evidence, Marx now tries to show in greater detail, what it is that the Hegelian type of an approach to the concrete ignores. For him, the Hegelians proceed in a "conduct" which "is merely speculative, merely theoretical"[59]. Although Marx had just shown that the concrete is not what it appears to be to the senses, but that it is a "concentration of many determinations hence the unity of the diverse", he also knows that it appears as such a "concentration" only "in the process of thinking". Such a conceptualization of the concrete is only the result of its mental analysis by the observer. However the concrete in itself has yet another way of being than serving for the theoretical approach as "the departure point of thinking". The study and understanding of "determinations" is only a "second path" for establishing the meaning of the concrete. The concrete has also an established meaning for those living it; and that one comes first.

Bearing this in mind, as according to Marx the economists of the 17th century did, one retains awareness for the circumstance that "along the second (path, FWS), the abstract determinations lead to the *reproduction* (my emphasis, FWS) of the concrete *by way of thought*" only (my emphasis, FWS). Ignoring this, "Hegel fell into the illusion of conceiving the real as the product of thought concentrating itself...". But, so Marx points out, "... rising from the abstract to the concrete is only the way in which thought appropriates the concrete... But this is by no means the process by which the concrete itself comes into being".

The mistake of the merely speculative mind is not simple, but, one might say, fittingly complex. First of all, the speculative mind ignores that there is, beside the dynamics in the speculative mind itself, also one in the minds of the people interacting out there and to be understood. Ignoring this implies a second mistake: the relationship between these two mind-sets is hardly ever explored by those with a speculative mind. Thirdly and more importantly, the real movement from the "thinnest abstractions" back to the concrete, i.e. to the concrete as it is enacted by life itself, is not viewed as a requirement

---

[59]A little later in this excerpt and on other occasions in this "Introduction", Marx elaborates on the limitations of the "theoretical method of appropriating the world" and on the precautions that such a method has to take. For comparative purposes see also: MEW I, 224, 384f; II, 60-62, 204; III, 167, 435; EB I, 327ff, 579.

for an adequate understanding on the part of the "speculative" researcher.

It needs to be noted though that when Marx illustrates the falsity of the Hegelian approach by using the "thinnest economic category ... exchange value" as an example, he does not mean to deny the a-priori-status of that category. He admits that "as a category ... exchange value leads an antediluvian existence". But *how* these abstractions existed for those enacting them, i.e. living them, is then still a matter in need of clarification. If one ignores this, a la Hegel, one is in quite some difficulties to explain economic reality. One would have to assume then that "the movement of the categories appears as the real act of production". This, of course, is materially impossible, unless one would resort to the assumption of "a jolt from the outside" that makes categories enact a praxis. Resorting to such an assumption, however, would render one's explanation of concrete praxis unfounded.

Having pointed out the absurdity of such an assumption, Marx reminds Hegel - and also the modern theoretical mind - that "the real subject (i.e. the agent behind the economic processes out there, FWS) retains its autonomous existence outside the head (of the researcher, FWS) just as before...". The attempt to comprehend it should, therefore, not at all start with the categories as they exist in the minds of the analysts and it should try to find out not only what the thinnest abstractions of a praxis are for the theoretical observer, but also what they are for the people in that praxis. Including them is the only way the theoretical method can hope to do justice to the circumstance that there is another "...subject, society..." out there "... as the presupposition...". If this presupposition is ignored, then the polit-economic research does not make sense.

Here, one has to bear in mind that Marx, while speaking about the "theoretical method", makes passing reference to other ways of "appropriating this world". What he has said so far in his "Method of Political Economy" was exclusively focussed on that "theoretical method" in whatever variation. However, the last eight to ten lines in this excerpt indicate that Marx does not only know of other methods of appropriating this world, namely "the artistic, religious, practical and mental" ones he also gives us a hint that he sees them as methods that are "a way different" from the "theoretical method". It would appear that his critique of the "theoretical method" would not apply to these non-theoretical methods. Are we then entitled to believe that "artistic, religious, practical and mental" approaches to this world, are not in the danger of ignoring that there are other human subjects as involved in the world out there as the theoretical mind is? An attempt to answer this question has to be made in a step by step fashion during our reading of later portions of the "Introduction".

Here, let us first note that Marx speaks among these "... different approaches to this world..." of the "practical and mental" one. I wonder whether the meaning of these adjectives is easily understood in the English translation. In the German original, the equivalent reads "*praktisch-geistig*", perhaps better translated as "practical-mental" than as "practical and mental". Marx refers here to the "mental", i.e. the thinking, directly involved in the praxis of doing, as opposed to the thinking of an outside observer, i.e. the one that would be "theoretical-mental". The translation "practical-mental" may help the English reader to see, more distinctly, the contrast between a praxis grounded appropriation of the world and a theoretical one. A "practical-mental" appropriation of the world is more than one that is just blindly grounded in praxis; it is knowingly grounded in praxis, i.e. it knows itself. This indicates that Marx is aware of a style of thinking in which the praxis can mentally appropriate itself, i.e. can be self-reflexive, self-critical, and thus can have the potential to transcend itself. Unfortunately, Marx does not tell us more about this style of thinking here, but he returns to it later[60].

At this stage, though, a few more of the theoretical concepts that Marx employs require our attention. Among them, the concept of "simple category" figures quite prominently. Marx's use of it is undoubtedly influenced by the Kantian heritage, and yet, as a

---

[60]See pp.92ff. See also MEW VII, 20. It should be clear that such an appropriation of praxis implies that thought cleanses itself of ideology and becomes truth; see MEW XVII, 343.

Dialectical Materialist, he conceives of it in a more subtle way than Kant did. This comes out in the next few pages of the "Introduction" from which the excerpts are taken that follow shortly.

First, let us note at this point that these excerpts and their focus on theoretical concepts indicate that Marx's own approach to the world is seen by him as a theoretical one as well. But it is one with a difference! The difference being, as has become visible already, that his approach does not ignore the interpretive subjectivities of those he wishes to understand, however critically so. His approach is willing to learn, and that is to say that it is willing to change itself and not to hang on to its preconceived categories. It is for this reason that I would suggest, as indicated above, that this section on "The Method of Political Economy" could be read as a Treatise on Learning.

Let us turn to one of these next excerpts as they focus on "labour". It reads:

p.103 Labour seems a quite simple category. The conception of labour in this general form - as labour as such - is also immeasurably old. Nevertheless, when it is economically conceived in this simplicity, 'labour' is as modern a category as are the relations which create this simple abstraction. The Monetary System[19], for example, still locates wealth altogether objectively, as an external thing, in money. Compared with this standpoint, the commercial, or manufacture, system
p.104 took a great step forward by locating the//source of wealth not in the object but in a subjective activity - in commercial and manufacturing activity - even though it still always conceives this activity within narrow boundaries, as money-making. In contrast to this system, that of the Physiocrats posits a certain kind of labour - agriculture - as the creator of wealth, and the object itself no longer appears in a monetary disguise, but as the product in general, as the general result of labour. This product, as befits the narrowness of the activity, still always remains a naturally determined

> product - the product of agriculture, the product of the earth *par excellence*.
> It was an immense step forward for Adam Smith to throw out every limiting specification of wealth-creating activity - not only manufacturing, or commercial or agricultural labour, but one as well as the others, labour in general. With the abstract universality of wealth-creating activity we now have the universality of the object defined as wealth, the product as such or again labour as such, but labour as past, objectified labour.
>
> > 19. Marx considered that the Monetary System, as defined here, covered economists from the sixteenth century to the Physiocrats. However, within the Monetary System there arose what he calls here the 'commercial, or manufacture system' but elsewhere the Mercantile System (known to economics textbooks as Mercantilism). He distinguishes between the two systems on pp. 327-8, but his normal practice is to link them together, since 'the Mercantile System is merely a variant of the Monetary System' (*A Contribution to the Critique of Political Economy*, London, 1971, p. 158)[61] (Marx's and the translator's italics, FWS).

First of all, we have to note that Marx speaks here of labour in terms of what it is not. He connects it to its result by seeing that result as "past, objectified labour". After having studied Part Two of this "Introduction", i.e. "The General Relation of Production to Distribution..." etc., we should be able to immediately see what Marx

---

[61] This explanatory footnote is added by the translator. It is not in the German undated edition.

is doing here: he defines a phenomenon in terms of its transcending other and the mediation between the two so that their "distinction in unity" comes into the open. But is Marx in doing so not contradicting his own objections against the "theoretical" or "speculative" mind? Is he not dogmatizing dialectics "theoretically" so that the essence of a postulated thesis is forced to appear in the light of its transcending other, i.e. its antithesis? I think that a careful analysis of the above excerpt will help us to answer this question and, implicitly, the question of what labor means as a "simple category".

Marx understands labor as a "simple category" which "in this general form", i.e. "as labour as such" is "immeasurably old", and yet "in this simplicity" it is also "as modern a category as ... the relations which create it" in "this simplicity". Does this not mean that Marx is able to see a commonality ("generality") in all labor ("immeasurably old" and yet "modern"), simply because he has the privilege of standing as a modern person at what has been so far the end of a historical process? Is it not exactly this that seems to mislead him into making a typically "theoretical" projection of the kind for which he has blamed others before? My answer to this question would be: not so! The reason for this response of mine is in part related to this and also, to some extent, to the next excerpt.

When we look at Marx's reasoning for this view on labor as a "simple category", we notice that he backs it up by taking three economic systems into consideration. They reach back to Mercantilism (see footnote 19 in the excerpt) and include the Physiocrats and Adam Smith's view on Capitalism. Even the oldest of these systems can hardly be considered "immeasurably old", and therefore does little to justify his concept of "labour as a simple category" to be "old" or even "antediluvian".

Yet there are two additional observations to be made here that are relevant to our understanding of this aspect in Marx's "Method".

On the one hand, Marx does not simply project his concept of labor into the two pre-capitalist formations that he inspects here, but he accepts their concept of labor. Let us note that he includes the conceptualization of those whom he wants to understand in his study. In doing this, he sees that it is not only he himself who conceptualizes labor in terms of something different from labor, but that the

Mercantilists themselves conceptualize labor (they do not "locate" it! The German equivalent for what is in the translation "locate" is "*setzen*", i.e. to assume or to postulate) as manifesting itself in "wealth", in "money", i.e. in something objective that is distinct from subjective labor, is even "external" to the latter. But the Mercantilists obviously do not see labor as synthesized in a transcending other (like labor is synthesized in capital under capitalist conditions), nor do they therefore explicate the mediation between labor and wealth, as Marx did for labor and capital at his time. Let us appreciate that Marx does not even once attempt to project a synthesis or a mediation into the Mercantilist views of labor and its result, obviously because such a synthesis and such a mediation were not seen by the Mercantilists and did not exist at the materially concrete level. That is to say labor was not yet "labor in general" and wealth was in fact not yet capital.

With the Physiocrats, the situation is quite similar in that they too understood labor in terms of its results, except that both labor and its physiocratically understood result, namely the "product of the earth", are even more narrowly and distinctively defined than the Mercantilists do under their conditions. The latter at least speak of all kinds of labor and then of wealth understood as money. But the Physiocrats speak "only" of agricultural labor, on the one hand and its products, namely agricultural produce, on the other. A dialectic between rural labor and foodstuff is not seen by the Physiocrats, and Marx does not project it "theoretically" into them.

On the other hand, Marx understands these two schools of economics and the life they describe as predecessors of capitalist praxis and theory. He has done this on other occasions as well[62]. Above, we saw how positively he speaks of the economists of the 17th century as opposed to those of his own century. Here, he indicates that he considers these pre-capitalist epochs as predecessors of Capitalism by writing that what Adam Smith had to say about labor in his time, particularly when Smith speaks of it as the creator of the "Wealth of Nations", "was an immense step forward". To be

---

[62]See e.g. MEW EB I, 529ff.

sure, Marx takes Smith's understanding of labor in Capitalism seriously, because he sees Smith's view as being founded in the materially concrete. Marx accepts Smith's view the same way as he had done with the definitions of labor given by the Mercantilists and Physiocrats, since their definitions had grown out of their reality. Marx's objections against Smith focus on something else, namely on Smith's non-critical, tacit acceptance of the materially concrete consequence of the relationship between labor and capital, namely: disaster. Marx sees and Smith suppresses acknowledgement of the circumstance that capital cannot help but run labor and thus itself into the ground. There is, however, no doubt in Marx's mind that Adam Smith sees capital as what it concretely is in Capitalism, namely "past, objectified labour". Smith's definition of labour (and thus of capital) is accepted by Marx, because labor had undergone a change at the materially concrete level: it had become labor without "every limiting specification"; it had concretely become "labour in general". Only as such and only in Capitalism could labor be defined in terms of an equally general opposite that transcended-and-contained that labor, namely as "past, objectified labor", i.e. as capital. The concrete reason for the possibility of such a definition is that "past, objectified labour" could only as capital retain its essence, namely invest itself always anew into the labor process, i.e. into production. Prior to Capitalism, a definition of labor in such terms would have been out of place. Only after the individuation of the bourgeois revolution could labor at the materially concrete level develop itself in a direction in the West that corresponded to the nature of capital. From then on labor had to be understood as what it had become, namely as having taken on a form that put it into a material-dialectic relation to capital[63].

It needs to be emphasized that this sense for the historical emergence of labor and capital implies a sense for the historicity of the form. It is in keeping with this implication that Marx does not simply project the concept of "general labor" backwards into the past. Certainly, he does see his concept of labor as already contained in the

---

[63]See also MEW IV, 475f, 483; EB I, 512ff, 520ff.

sense that was rightfully made of labor in previous epochs, and he certainly sees that the concept of capitalist "general labour" could be related therefore to previous more limited forms of labor, but he dares to make the conceptual relation only because "general labour" has developed out of these earlier forms at the materially-concrete level, meaning that he conceptualizes that evolvement (and therefore his projection) only where that evolvement has concretely occurred. It is for this same reason, so we have to stress, that the connection that he makes between the present and the past in this regard is not one of the usual "theoretical" projections either. It is a projection all right, and it is a theoretical one, but unlike a Hegelian projection, it is grounded in a materially concrete historical process. This is also to say that we arrive here again at an insight which we had to note before, namely that Dialectical Materialism and its concepts are historically *relative* to a particular materially concrete praxis. So we see that the historical projection of Dialectic-Materialist concepts is permissible at best within the historical tradition out of which Capitalism and Dialectical Materialism were born, and nowhere else[64].

I would suggest that the next excerpt will help to clarify further Marx's Dialectic-Materialist way of thinking. We have an opportunity to observe his way of "theoretically appropriating the world", as he delivers another treatment of "general labour", this time, however, by focusing on yet another aspect of it.

p.104 Indifference towards any specific kind of labour presupposes a very developed totality of real kinds of labour, of which no single one is any longer predominant. As a rule, the most general abstractions arise only in the midst of the richest possible concrete development, where one thing appears as common to many, to all. Then it ceases to be thinkable in a

[64]This expresses itself not only in explicit statements as presented above for instance on pp. 17ff, but also in Marx's concept of the uniqueness of the proletariat, see MEW III, 67ff; IV, 473ff.

particular form alone. On the other side, this abstraction of labour as such is not merely the mental product of a concrete totality of labours. Indifference towards specific labours corresponds to a form of society in which individuals can with ease transfer from one labour to another, and where the specific kind is a matter of chance for them, hence of indifference. Not only the category, labour, but labour in reality has here become the means of creating wealth in general, and has ceased to be organically linked with particular individuals in any specific form. Such a state of affairs is at its most developed in the most modern form of existence of bourgeois society - in the United States. Here, then,//for the first time, the point of departure of modern economics, namely the abstraction of the category 'labour', 'labour as such', labour pure and simple, becomes true in practice. The simplest abstraction, then, which modern economics places at the head of its discussions, and which expresses an immeasurably ancient relation valid in all forms of society, nevertheless achieves practical truth as an abstraction only as a category of the most modern society. One could say that this indifference towards particular kinds of labour, which is a historic product in the United States, appears e.g. among the Russians as a spontaneous inclination. But there is a devil of a difference between barbarians who are fit by nature to be used for anything, and civilized people who apply themselves to everything. And then in practice the Russian indifference to the specific character of labour corresponds to being embedded by tradition within a very specific kind of labour, from which only external influences can jar them loose.

p.105

This example of labour shows strikingly how even the most abstract categories, despite their validity - precisely because of their abstractness - for all epochs, are nevertheless, in the specific character of this

> abstraction, themselves likewise a product of historic relations, and possess their full validity only for and within these relations.

Let me begin my commentary on this excerpt by starting out, for a change, with its last sentence.

I think, in it, Marx makes two points by, as is typical for his way of thinking, tracing the concrete dialectic between them. The first and seemingly simple point is that "the most abstract categories..." have "...their validity... for all epochs...", i.e. there is a commonality or unity among them. Then he protects this point against a potential "Hegelian" interpretation by the second point.

This second point, however, is much more complex and its inspection will take up considerable space here.

Marx, though, makes that point with the relative simplicity that can only be attained by those who have a sense for the dialectics of the materially concrete. While Marx does speak here of the distinction in that unity, he first points out that that unity is understood along a historical dimension and not along a dimension of simultaneity as was the case above, for instance, in the unity between production, consumption, distribution and exchange.

Marx refers to this historical connection, when he writes that "the most abstract categories ... possess their full validity only for ... relations" which are "likewise a product of historical relations". This, I think makes it clear that Marx does not speak about abstract categories and their relations in a transcultural and/or universalistic sense. He speaks very consciously of them as products of a historically concrete connectedness. It is for the reason of this concrete historical connection that the most abstract categories, "in the specific character" (the German says here "*in der Bestimmtheit*", i.e. "in their determination", FWS) of this abstraction "have validity ... for all epochs". These categories are general, not because they are projections of the "theoretical" mind, but because they form a concrete historical unity, although one in distinction.

Marx identifies this distinction in unity even at two levels, namely at the objective and the subjective level of those involved. This emphasizes all the more that acknowledging the unity of the abstract category labor between an old (Russia) and a modern (U.S.) mode of production does not at all imply the sameness of this category within the two. The reason for the distinction within the category of labor in the U.S. and Russia does not just lie with it being objectively embedded in different totalities, Marx also sees the apparent sameness of the subjective attitude, namely "the indifference towards labour" among Russians and Americans, and yet points out that this is a commonality in distinction as well. Furthermore, Marx avoids to segregate the subjective from the objective level. This is to say that Marx makes a statement on the historical nature of individuals' consciousness by keeping it related to the materially concrete forms of production. In other words, this way he compares two kinds of "indifference towards any specific kind of labour", one which, in the case of the U.S. "presupposes a very developed totality of real kinds of labour" and a second one which, in the case of Russia," ... corresponds to being embedded by tradition within a very specific kind of labour...". On top of all this Marx bears in mind that the Russian and the American forms of production are historically and thus concretely related; they belong both to Western history.

I am skeptical, though, whether the English translation of how Marx understands the Russian case of indifference allows the reader to fully understand what Marx means to say in this connection. The German text does not just say that Russians are "embedded" in "a very specific kind of labour"; it uses a much stronger metaphor which is admittedly quite hard to translate, namely "*Festgerittensein*". Nonetheless, the German original means that the Russians are "stuck" (not only "embedded") in "a very specific kind of labour" and says that their being stuck is a matter of tradition, i.e. they are traditionally stuck.

Marx contrasts this with labor in the most modern society in the West where "... individuals can with ease transfer from one labour to another, and where the specific kind is a matter of chance for them, hence of indifference. Not only the category, labour, but labour in reality has become here the means of creating wealth in general (i.e. capital, FWS) and has ceased to be organically linked with particular individuals ...". In other words, individuals *are* no longer carpenters, bricklayers, miners etc., they simply do a job, be it this one or that one[65].

By focusing even more narrowly on the connection between consciousness and the level of social development, Marx continues this way: "One could say that this indifference towards particular kinds of labour, which is a historic product in the United States, appears e.g. among the Russians as a spontaneous inclination. But there is a devil of a difference...". While emphasizing the commonality between the indifference towards labor in the U.S. and Russia, he introduces his awareness of the distinction between these two kinds of indifference rather strongly. I think the key concepts in the introduction of this distinction are "historic product" and "spontaneous inclination". Unfortunately though, both these key concepts require some explanation, since they are not very well translated.

"Spontaneous inclination" does not carry the meaning of what are the supposedly translated words of the German text, namely "*naturwüchsige Anlage*". "Inclination" as a translation of "*Anlage*" is problematic, since "*Anlage*" means "inborn disposition", "inborn gift" or "talent". As such, a gift or a talent may constantly retain a state of preparedness in a person for doing something, but an inborn gift is not itself an inclination; a gift while being constantly there, gives one an inclination to do something now and not then. Additionally, Marx speaks of this "*Anlage*", i.e. this gift, as being "*naturwüchsig*", i.e. grown by nature and that is to say, by nature alone. This, however, is a term that Marx uses, most of the time and certainly here, in order to indicate that something qualified by that adjective is only *seen* as a nature grown phenomenon, while in reality it is not nature grown, but a social creation and thus changeable[66].

The problems of the English translation become even greater, since they are compounded with the use of "spontaneous" for "*na-*

---

[65]See MEW XXIII, 512f where a first hand account on labor in the U.S. is quoted.

[66]Compare to MEW I, 369; II, 127f; III, 31ff, 37, 60-73; IV, 139; IX, 132; XIX, 317; EB I, 535ff; see also "*Grundrisse*", 111.

turwüchsig". As we saw above, the concepts of "spontaneity" and "spontaneous" occupy a very specific place in the Critical Tradition. They are closely connected with man's true nature. But Marx means to say here that the talent that seems to be inborn into the Russian soul is only in appearance inborn, i.e. spontaneous or nature given. In other words, the English translation confuses, at this point, the meaning of the German original completely.

Let us remember that, after all, the "indifference" of Russian labor is understood by Marx as grounded, even "stuck", in tradition, while the American one has grown out of tradition. This is to say that, in reality, the "indifference" towards labor is in both cases not nature grown at all, it only looks like that to the uncritical mind, be it that of the "theoretical" observer or of those practically involved in that labor. However, the distinction between the American and the Russian "indifference towards labour" relates to their different position in history. The American indifference is a very young, i.e. the most recent product of history. It is, therefore, quite obviously a "historic product", as Marx says in the text, while the Russian tradition is so old, as if it had been there always, so that it, therefore, appears to be given by nature. It remains to be seen, however, whether it is only the Russian and not also the American form of labor that has a (false) sense about itself as being grown by nature. In other words, there may be a commonality in distinction as well regarding the false consciousness about the indifference towards labor between the Russian and American labor.

The sentence after the one on the "spontaneous inclination" perpetuates, in the English translation, the mistake of the previous one. It sounds as if people in less developed societies were "fit by nature", seemingly by true and undistorted nature, "... to be used for anything". The German text, however, says that it makes "a devil of a difference, whether barbarians have the gift" ("*Anlage*" FWS) - notabene the gift that Marx has just characterized as being falsely perceived as a gift by Mother Nature - "to be used for anything". I think that Marx uses the passive tense of "to be used" quite consciously in connection with the Russians, since it allows him to contrast their "indifference towards labour" with that of the

Americans, where "... people..." actively "...apply themselves to everything".

Furthermore, the difference between the two forms of labor is not only related to the passiveness of the Russian "indifference towards labour", but also and more importantly, as Marx says in the sentence that follows in this excerpt, labor in Russia is "traditionally stuck (remember my correction of the translation! FWS) in a quite specific labour" so that "only external influences can jar them loose". This is to say that for Marx the barbarian "indifference" goes that far that people cannot even liberate themselves from their traditionally, i.e. perpetually accepted roles. There is certainly a unity in the indifference towards labor between the U.S. American and Russian society, but the distinction is that in the latter case the "indifference" itself is stuck with "the specific character of labour", while in the former the "indifference" towards labor "is a matter of chance".

While Marx characterizes two distinct and yet comparable subjective attitudes towards labor in this excerpt, he could still be misunderstood in yet another regard. Readers might think that Marx accepts the modern kind of "indifference" uncritically. Certainly, being willingly involved in one's performance is seen by him as a product of history, i.e. of progress, but that is by no means to say that he approves of capitalist labor, or what appears to be its happy acceptance of the diversity of jobs. Of course, we have to reach beyond the limits of the present text in order to remember his position on this[67]. He knows that as long as modern labor has that happy understanding of itself as being free in its relation to capital, labor in Capitalism has a false consciousness too, in this case, about the essence of capital as an unavoidably exploitative instrument. Modern false consciousness is certainly distinct from the old one, but it has still a strong commonality with it: they both falsely accept their

[67]It is, of course, central to Marx's whole understanding of capital as a social relation that capital is destructive to labor and that labor, therefore, cannot afford to find Capitalism acceptable. For passages in which Marx explicitly rejects such an acceptance, see MEW II, 37; IV, 475f; XXIII, 281f, 511f; EB I, 512ff.

indifference towards labor and their mode of production as nature grown.

As far as labor in today's Late Capitalist mode of production is concerned, it is for us to observe and to judge whether that kind of labor, which has even a greater variety of jobs available for itself than was the case in the U.S. over 100 years ago, ignores the commonality in the distinctiveness of these jobs, namely the exploitation prevailing in all of them. The question then is, "can" modern labor "jar itself loose" from that circumstance? And one might also wonder, whether that historical task is of a lesser order in modern society than the one that labor had to confront under less developed conditions. The questions even arise whether it is nowadays still only "labor" that has to "jar itself loose" from being exploited and whether exploitation has not taken on a meaning that Marx could not and did not dream of.

With these considerations and questions, I would like to leave my commentary on the excerpt taken from the pages 104 and 105 of the "Introduction" behind.

The remainder of the "Introduction" is, to a large extent, devoted to the question of how one can understand past societies from the standpoint of the present, i.e. from the standpoint of the bourgeois society. Marx discusses three different aspects of historical understanding in these paragraphs. It is in accordance with these aspects that I selected three excerpts from these pages. Two of these excerpts shed additional light on the "theoretical" mind and also on the "practical-mental appropriation of the world", while the last excerpt (which also ends the "Introduction") focusses on the artistic mode of understanding. Considering, however, that each of these three excerpts could be viewed as implying a notion of general evolutionism, it may be appropriate to address the question again, whether Marx believed that the concepts gained from his critical examination of bourgeois society were applicable, in his mind, to the study of any society, i.e. were of general validity.

While it should be clear by now that my answer to this question is unequivocally negative, it must still be admitted that Marx came only gradually in the course of his life to consciously reject the "general", or better, the "transhistorical" or "transcultural" applicability of his thought. Certainly after the inspection of the excerpts taken from pp. 103/4 and 104/5 of the "Introduction", it is fair to say that Marx already limits the claim for the applicability of his concepts to that tradition which is concretely related to, and ends up in, the development of bourgeois society. I would also like to point out that Marx, on these final pages of the "Introduction", quite rarely makes reference to modes of production that lie outside the Western tradition. In the excerpt taken from p. 106 of the "Introduction" (presented here on pp. 92ff), he briefly mentions "oriental economics". However, he rejects the inclusion of "mere hunting and fishing peoples", since they "lie outside the point where real development begins" as he says later in the "Introduction", namely on p. 107 (not excerpted here). And yet, I cannot deny that earlier in this section on "The Method of Political Economy", i.e. at the bottom of p. 102 (not excerpted here either), Marx refers to another definitely non-Western society, namely that of Pre-Columbian Peru. He undoubtedly applies concepts that clearly derive from Western Political Economy, like "economy", "co-operation", "money", "exchange", to this Ancient Empire and thus treats Inca-Peru as an example of the "less mature forms of society". So, what are we to make out of this? Does this not revive the question again whether Marx was a generalist in the usual sense of the word?

Let me say that my answer to this question as it comes up again through the reading of this text is still the same as the one given above[68]. This is to say, I believe that the Marx of 1857/8, i.e. of the time of writing this "Introduction", had not yet fully appreciated what his own reasoning already contained. This appreciation came to his full awareness only later in his life. It seems to be advisable to keep this development in Marx's own thinking in mind, when we now embark on our inspection of the last three excerpts taken from this "Introduction". We read:

p.105 Bourgeois society is the most developed and the most complex historical organization of production. The

---

[68]See also pp. 17ff and footnotes 22, 23.

> categories which express its relations, the comprehension of its structure, thereby also allows insights into the structure and the relations of production of all the vanished social formations out of whose ruins and elements it built itself up, whose partly still unconquered remnants are carried along within it, whose mere nuances have developed explicit significance within it, etc. Human anatomy contains a key to the anatomy of the ape. The intimations of higher development among the subordinate animal species, however, can be understood only after the higher development is already known. The bourgeois economy thus supplies the key to the ancient, etc. But not at all in the manner of those economists who smudge over all historical differences and see bourgeois relations in all forms of society. One can understand tribute, tithe, etc., if one is acquainted with ground rent. But one must not identify them.

I think that the last three sentences of this excerpt make it again perfectly clear that Marx does not at all advocate the typically "theoretical" projection of the present into the past, not even when staying within one and the same tradition. He sees the present as endowed with the ability to understand the past, because the present is a product of the past in the sense of being in a state of greater differentiation than the past "whose mere nuances have developed explicit significance within" the present. This is to say that Marx is aware of the methodological advantage of hindsight. We, living in the present, know what was a yet unknown future for the past. It, however, remains an important condition for a proper understanding of the past that one does not simply identify what has "explicit significance" in the present with what was still undifferentiated in the past. As Marx sees it here, the advantage of having hindsight can turn easily into a problem where the distinctions in identity are not seen. Simple projections of the present into the past will indeed preclude proper understanding[69]. And yet, avoidance of sheer projection is only one of the important conditions for understanding the past. Another one is self-critique to be learned from the criticalness and self-critique of those historical stages to be understood. This comes out in the next excerpt which implicitly sheds light on the "practical-mental" way of understanding and what it can teach the "theoretical way of appropriating the world".

> p.106 The so-called historical presentation of development is founded, as a rule, on the fact that the latest form regards the previous ones as steps leading up to itself, and, since it is only rarely and only under quite specific conditions able to criticize itself - leaving aside, of course, the historical periods which appear to themselves as times of decadence - it always conceives them one-sidedly. The Christian religion was able to be of assistance in reaching an objective understanding of earlier mythologies only when its own self-criticism had been accomplished to a certain degree, so to speak, *dynamie*. Likewise, bourgeois economics arrived at an understanding of feudal, ancient, oriental economics only after the self-criticism of bourgeois society had begun. In so far as the bourgeois economy did not mythologically identify itself altogether with the past, its critique of the previous economies, notably of feudalism, with which it was still engaged in direct struggle, resembled the critique which Christianity levelled against paganism, or also that of Protestantism against Catholicism.

This excerpt obviously takes off from the problematic aspect of hindsight. We read, in the first sentence, that the "historical presentation of development" is carried out by the "latest forms" of societies, "as a rule" in two, certainly dubious ways. On the one

---

[69]See also MEW III, 113f, 167; IV, 140; VIII, 114.

hand, the "latest form (of societies, FWS) regard the previous ones as steps leading up to itself" - which, however, the previous ones could only objectively do but not subjectively know! - and on the other, such a "latest form ...always conceives them", i.e. the previous ones, "onesidedly", i.e. without doing justice to them. This is to say that the "theoretical" understanding of the past suffers from projecting its own knowledge and categories as "antediluvian" ones into the past. Marx also states, in this connection, that a "latest form" is "only rarely and only under quite specific conditions able to criticise itself", obviously implying that self-critique would be a condition for adequate understanding, meaning in the present context, the understanding of the past. Marx also seems to express here that self-critique, while being a condition for understanding, has conditions of its own. He says of them that they are "rare and quite specific". We are not told how many conditions he has in mind and what all of them are. At any rate, he explicates two of them.

Marx identifies one of these conditions in the hyphenated subclause of this excerpt. He seems to suggest there that those "historical periods which appear to themselves as times of decadence", i.e. which know of their state of crisis, have the ability to critique themselves and thus to understand past forms of society. The second and the third sentence of this excerpt give us examples in which self-critique has, in fact, lead to an ability to understand. Christianity could understand "earlier mythologies" after "its own self-criticism ("self-critique" would have been a more adequate translation, FWS) had been accomplished to a certain degree". And "(L)ikewise bourgeois economics arrived at an understanding" of other economics "after the self-criticism of bourgeois society had begun". The attainment of this latter ability is, not the least, demonstrated in Marx's own critique of bourgeois society. He has documented, e.g. in the earlier parts of this "Introduction", how he could unveil the mystifying consequences that bourgeois conceptions of the past had, if they were, without self-critique, simply projected into the past. Let us emphasize what Marx is saying here: it is a condition for understanding the past that one is engaged in the critique of one's own praxis. This implies the mental awareness of the praxis of one's own epoch, i.e. is a "practical-mental appropriation of the world" one lives in. This appropriation, however, has its own condition. The critique of bourgeois economics as delivered by Marx became possible, i.e. had its condition in the circumstance that the decadence of that system had become visible in the materially-concrete misery that it had created. Had that critique induced a commonly practiced self-critique of Capitalism, that whole mode of production would have had a chance to understand the past in understanding itself. Another example for gaining the ability to understand is Christianity. It too had, undoubtedly, come into serious problems, e.g. prior to the Reformation, before it learned to look at itself critically and thus to be of assistance in reaching an "objective understanding of earlier mythologies"[70].

Another condition for gaining the abilities of critiquing and understanding arises, when social formations are young, not at all in a state of decadence, but on the move of ascendance. This is brought out in the last sentence of this excerpt. Marx says that there was a time "when the bourgeois economy did not mythologically identify itself ... with the past ...", i.e. it did not do yet what it did later, namely project its own concepts into other formations. The avoidance of such projection occurred at a time when bourgeois society "was still engaged in direct struggle ... notably with feudalism". At that time, it understood itself as a critique of that past with which it still identified itself. At the point of that historical change, bourgeois society understood itself in a "practical-mental" way and thus had a chance to learn how to understand otherness - in this case feudalism - in distinction from itself. Christianity was in the same state of consciousness when it grew out of its critique of paganism (or Judaism, FWS) and so was Protestantism in its early struggle with Catholicism.

In other words, new social forms in their very early stages, and old forms in their stages of decadence are in a state of practical critique. These are the historical moments at which new emerging and old dying social formations have the "rare and quite specific opportunity" to learn how to see new formations within the old one and thus to

---

[70]See also MEW I, 385.

understand the otherness of the latter without "mythologically identifying themselves with the past". Mature established social forms prior to their decadence and self-critique simply believe in themselves and are, therefore, incapable of and unable to understand.

As an aside I would like to raise a question here that focusses on Marx's personality. His earlier years were a critique of Dialectical Idealism and bourgeois praxis. He saw both in decadence and yet was part of them. His critique of them was his struggle with himself. In that process he arrived at a determinate negation of what he was about to outgrow. In his middle years Marx came to believe in his own theory firmly enough to tendentially assume its overriding, i.e. general, applicability. Thus he put himself somewhat in the danger of failing at the task of understanding. But in his old age, he saw his own thought in its own limitations and thus came to disclaim its general, i.e. "super-historical" validity. As we saw above, however, instead of sensing it as wrong, he saw that it had been geared to a particular life-form, namely that of bourgeois society, and thus he noticed that other social forms demanded other sets of conceptual tools for their understanding; these had to be different from the ones Dialectical Materialism provided. These tools had to grow with the critical understanding of these other social forms. This finally made him see what was implicit in his thinking already during his earlier years, namely the primacy of nature over thinking. Let us note again here that Marx refers to the primacy of nature over thinking and not to the primacy of the *concept* of nature over thinking[71]. The question of how Marx suggests to practice the primacy of nature over thinking will be dealt with in our inspection of the final paragraphs of this "Introduction". At the present juncture, I simply wish to emphasize that an awareness for the primacy of nature and thus for the critique of his own "theoretical approach" had already taken shape in his mind during his work on the "*Grundrisse*".

---

[71]See above pp. xf.

4.- Celebrating Art: The Sensuality of Understanding

At the twilight of his life, as we had reason to mention before[72], he could put his earlier thinking into its place and reason against its dogmatization more clearly than he could do in earlier periods. And yet, a strong appreciation for the strength of approaching the world in a way that is more directly grounded in nature comes to light in the final paragraphs of this "Introduction". There he writes about art and its way of relating to the world[73]. It seems that, for Marx, that kind of understanding has no difficulties in granting distinct subjectivity to a previous epoch out of which the present one has grown. Art seems to be a living appreciation of what he had theorized about in terms of distinction in unity.

Let us turn to that portion of the text that is of relevance in this connection.

p.110 (1) In the case of the arts, it is well known that certain periods of their flowering are out of all proportion to the general development of society, hence also to the material foundation, the skeletal structure as it were, of its organization. For example, the Greeks compared to the moderns or also Shakespeare. It is even recognized that certain forms of art, e.g. the epic, can no longer be

---

[72]See again pp. 17ff and footnotes 22, 23.

[73]Marx's appreciation of art, so often ignored, has in fact accompanied his entire life. It would be impossible to do justice to this circumstance by listing a few references. Let it suffice to point out that his doctoral dissertation of 1841 would be losing considerably without its references to art (see e.g. MEW EB I, 283); that "The Capital" has its good share of references to art; and that finally his correspondence with Vera Zasulitsch (1881) borrows from poetry and drama (e.g. Ibsen). It is well known that Marx liked to tell stories paraphrasing Shakespeare's plays to his children on Sunday walks with them. Finally, one should perhaps remember that Marx had contemplated in the early 1840s to write on religious art together with Bruno Bauer.

produced in their world epoch-making, classical stature as soon as the production of art, as such, begins; that is, that certain significant forms within the realm of the arts are possible only at an undeveloped stage of artistic development. If this is the case with the relation between different kinds of art within the realm of the arts, it is already less puzzling that it is the case in the relation of the entire realm to the general development of society. The difficulty consists only in the general formulation of these contradictions. As soon as they have been specified, they are already clarified.

Let us take e.g. the relation of Greek art and then of Shakespeare to the present time. It is well known that Greek mythology is not only the arsenal of Greek art but also its foundation. Is the view of nature and of social relations on which the Greek imagination and hence Greek [mythology] is based possible with self-acting mule spindles and railways and locomotives and electrical telegraphs? What chance has Vulcan against Roberts & Co., Jupiter against the lightning-rod and Hermes against the Credit Mobilier? All mythology overcomes and dominates and shapes the forces of nature in the imagination and by the imagination; it therefore vanishes with the advent of real mastery over them. What becomes of Fama alongside Printing House Square? Greek art presupposes Greek mythology, i.e. nature and the social forms already reworked in an unconsciously artistic way by the popular imagination. This is its material. Not any mythology whatever, i.e. not an arbitrarily chosen unconsciously artistic reworking of nature (here meaning everything objective, hence including society). Egyptian mythology could never have been the foundation or the womb of Greek art. But, in any case, a *mythology*. Hence, in no way a social development which excludes all mythological, all mythologizing relations to nature; which therefore demands of the artist an imagination not dependent on mythology.

p.111 From another side: is Achilles possible with powder and lead? Or the *Iliad* with the printing press, not to mention the printing machine? Do not the song and the saga and the muse necessarily come to an end with the printer's bar, hence do not the necessary conditions of epic poetry vanish?

But the difficulty lies not in understanding that the Greek arts and epic are bound up with certain forms of social development. The difficulty is that they still afford us artistic pleasure and that in a certain respect they count as a norm and as an unattainable model.

A man cannot become a child again, or he becomes childish. But does he not find joy in the child's naïveté, and must he himself not strive to reproduce its truth at a higher stage? Does not the true character of each epoch come alive in the nature of its children? Why should not the historic childhood of humanity, its most beautiful unfolding, as a stage never to return, exercise an eternal charm? There are unruly children and precocious children. Many of the old peoples belong in this category. The Greeks were normal children. The charm of their art for us is not in contradiction to the undeveloped stage of society on which it grew. [It] is its result, rather, and is inextricably bound up, rather, with the fact that the unripe social conditions under which it arose, and could alone arise, can never return (Marx's italics, FWS).

It may be worth noting that we have, with the above excerpt, left Section Three of the "Introduction" behind. We are now in the rather short and apparently incomplete Section Four which abruptly finishes the "Introduction". I also want it to be noted that I am not able to do justice to all aspects of art referred to in these paragraphs. All I can do here is stick to those aspects in Marx's considerations which have some relevance for his notion of those "rare and quite specific conditions" which allow a "latest form" of development to understand and critique itself and its predecessors.

Marx takes off from the observation that art sometimes, e.g. among the ancient Greeks, and also in Shakespeare's hands, flowers "out of all proportion to the general development of society...", and its "...material foundation...(C)ertain forms of art, e.g. the epic..." are created then that "...can no longer be produced in their world epoch-making, classical stature as soon as the production of art, as such, begins...", i.e. when art has differentiated itself as a separate activity distinct from all others. It is important for us to note that Marx understands the disparities between the development of art and that of social organization as contradictions. But, he also says about these contradictions that "(A)s soon as they have been specified, they are already clarified".

Marx clarifies these contradictions by demonstrating that the Greek imagination and mythology which are the "foundation" and "arsenal" of Greek art cannot go together with modern man's domination of nature; *that* would be a contradiction, and not the conjunction of great mythological art and poor social development. "All mythology overcomes ... the forces of nature in the imagination ..., it therefore vanishes with the advent of real mastery over them". "(A)longside Printing House Square", "Fama" has as little room as Achilles would have in a world "with powder and lead" (let alone one with lasers and laser guided missiles). The "classical stature" of Greek art cannot be explained out of the economic base of Greek society; it is not and cannot be a mirrorlike reflexion of that base. And yet, it is its true superstructure, because that art is a naive product of a people's imagination, better yet, an imagination in longing, and that is a wholehearted longing of a whole people united in that longing. This, I think is meant when Marx writes: "Greek art presupposes Greek mythology", meaning that Greek art presupposes "... nature and the social forms (going with it, FWS) already reworked in an unconsciously artistic way by the popular imagination". As an

Idea, Greek art is not an ideology that makes the concretely existing underdevelopment bearable (and thus prolongs it by serving as an opiate). As an Idea, Greek art projects a longed-for utopia out of a concrete situation, if not into heaven, then, onto the heights of the Olympus. It is out of this concrete utopia that the ancient Greek could both understand and critique their concrete life situation.

This ancient utopia is a jointly and unconsciously created product of the people. Not only are the social conditions for such creativity gone today, "the unripe social conditions under which it arose, and could alone, arise, can never return". "But the difficulty lies not in the understanding that the Greek arts and epic are bound up with certain forms of social development. The difficulty is that they still afford us artistic pleasure and that in a certain respect they count as a norm and as an unattainable model". Given the past, i.e. given what has happened to us since ancient times, we have lost the innocence of dreaming together. Of course, would modern man dream the way the ancient Greeks did, he would become childish. But on the other hand, as an adult,"... does he not find joy in the child's naivete, and must he himself not strive to reproduce its truth at a higher stage?"

Marx's answer to this rhetorical question is clearly a "yes". This affirmation has two aspects embedded in it. First, Greek mythology was obviously true, and second, it was not true consciously. This is to say, Greek mythology and Folk art were true, but the ancient Greek had no conscious awareness of themselves; modern man has a consciousness of himself, but he is false[74]. The truth of Greek folk art and mythology rested with the togetherness of the people with one another in their shared mythology and it rested also with their relationship to nature, as it was understood in that mythology. To the extent that these ways of knowing were direct, i.e. without a self-distancing reflexion, they were naive[75].

---

[74]Regarding false consciousness in Capitalism, see MEW I, 346, 579; II, 55ff; III, 30ff, 233; VIII, 139f; IX, 225.

[75]I am using the word "*naive*" in the sense in which Goethe and Schiller have understood it. I believe that Marx uses that adjective here in the same way, at least this is what the context suggests to me. Unfortunately, I am

It would be important to note that Marx does not discuss questions here related to sheer correctness of Greek natural science. The truth of their knowledge rests for him with the socially shared groundedness of that knowledge of nature, and with the obvious circumstance that that knowledge helped them to live off nature and to live in harmony with nature and among themselves. This appears to be sufficient for Marx's concept of truth.

But, it is a naive truth. "At a higher stage", i.e., in the 19th century, man's truth will still have to be grounded in nature, otherwise truth would not be concrete. Given our historical journey and our march through the purgatory of rationalism, this truth has, however, imploded into sheer correctness; a correctness which in the impoverishment of modern epistemology is grounded in the strategic notion of our successes in the manipulation of nature out there and in our fellow human beings. This correctness, and the concomitant strategism of our thinking, distances us from nature in ourselves and "out there" and, because of the individuation that goes with rationalism, this way of thinking distances us from one another. Therefore, our kind of correctness can no longer be naive. A future truth, should it ever grow out of the determinate negation of this correctness, will not be naive in the Greek sense either, but it will be a conscious one.

And yet, modern man, his rationalism notwithstanding, is still aesthetically captivated by Greek art, at least he was in Marx's day and age. That is to say that via an organ neglected in the distorted thinking of modernity, namely "artistic pleasure", we can relate to

---

not able to make references to other passages in Marx's writings where he uses the word "*naive*" in the same way as he seems to do that here. Unpacking the meaning of the Goethe-Schiller-concept "*naive*" would hardly be possible within this commentary. In very broad terms, one could perhaps say that "*naive*" meant in that tradition something like acting out of one's undistorted nature (spontaneity) without any instrumentalistic intent. The best way to appropriate the meaning of that concept would be by reading Schiller's "*Über naive und sentimentalische Dichtung*" ("On naive and sentimental poetry") in: *Schillers Sämtliche Werke, Säkular-Ausgabe* in 16 *Bänden*, Stuttgart (Cotta), 1904-05. See there vol. 12.

ancient truth. As we saw Marx write "...the Greek arts and epic ... still afford us artistic pleasure and ... count as a norm and as an unattainable model". In other words, the artistic pleasure, a definitely sensual phenomenon, ties even us moderns together, although our individuated self-consciousness does not yet allow us to appreciate our own bodily nature as the condition for that commonly shared pleasure. But we long for that pleasure; it turns ancient art into a model for us. Marx does not say anything here about the question of how an appreciation of our bodily commonality would potentially affect our knowledge of nature. For him, our inner nature is, so I strongly believe , not only a commonality among all of us, as it can express itself in shared pleasure, our inner nature is also the condition for our new knowledge of nature and for our new understanding of other human beings. Since his "Theses on Feuerbach", it goes indeed without saying for him that it is only because we all are of this world that we can know this world and can relate to one another. Putting this into Kantian language, we could say that our nature makes up the categoriality not only of our theorizing but also of our praxis. This means, now transcending Kant, that the commonality of nature can not only reunite man the thinker with man the doer - who had fallen apart in Kant's philosophy - , but, if we allow our inner nature, i.e. our spontaneous will, to give us insight into this unity, it will also imply the pleasure of sensing the unity of all beings in distinction[76].

---

[76]I believe that this thought of Marx's is nowhere better expressed than in a passage that we find in the "Economic-Philosophical Manuscripts" of 1844, see MEW EB I, 544. We read: "The whole of history is preparatory history so that man can become an object of the *sensual* consciousness ... History itself is a *real* part of nature's history, of its evolvement up to the inclusion of man. Later on, the natural science will in as much subsume the science of man as the science of man will subsume the natural science: it will be *one* science... *Man* is the immediate (*unmittelbare*) object of the natural science, since the immediate *sensual* nature is for man the immediately human sensuality... as the other human being exists immediately for him sensually, since his own sensuality exists for him as human sensuality only through other human beings. But *nature* is the immediate object of the science of man. The foremost object of man - man

This commonality would grant each of us our uniqueness and save us from sameness. Or, in other words, a sensual appreciation - not the theoretical concept - of the commonality of matter within each of us, among all of us, and with that matter around us could resurrect "at a higher stage" the naivete of the ancient Greek. They too knew this commonality, though in a mythological way, it was their truth. It is for us to regain ours.

It is from here that we can return to the problem of understanding. The art of understanding would reach an entirely new quality, far beyond what the "theoretical mind" is capable of, would our self-consciousness return to nature. Then neither the other, nor self, nor nature out there would be alien to us. We would know their identity as it mediates the world including mankind in 1001 forms; and even the way of our knowing that identity would be part of that mediation.

In my reading, the "Introduction" of the "*Grundrisse*" culminates in these considerations. It would be our task now to unfold how Marx describes capital as a social relation that constantly crushes the emergence of the new naivete[77]. So much, however, can be said about it at this point already. Capital as the onesided appropriation of "past, objectified labor" is a materially-concrete contradiction to labor; it exploits labor. Capital, however, cannot admit to that and has, therefore, to lie about itself as a relationship to labor. This lie implies that the superstructure of capitalist society, i.e. its whole culture, can never really call anything by its proper name. The spontaneity, as it underlies truth and ties us into the rest of nature,

---

- is nature, sensuality, and the particular human sensual forces of his essence, as they can find their objectified (*gegenständliche*) realization only in *natural* objects, can only find knowledge of themselves (*ihre Selbsterkenntnis*) in the science of man as a natural creature. The element of thinking itself, the element of the living externalization of thought, language, is itself of a sensual nature. The *social* reality of nature and the *human* natural science or the natural science of man are identical expressions" (my translation, FWS).

[77]Capital is for Marx *the* negation of our true nature. Therefore, capital is the negation that must be negated, see e.g. MEW XXIII, 291.

has to be distorted by capital in every way possible. This is to say that the superstructure of Capitalism can only be ideology. In view of the appreciation that Marx had for the "artistic way of appropriating the world", at least on an occasion like the one we have studied here, some of us may think that Marx may not have been so convinced that a theoretical approach could dissolve the veils that surround the nature of things in Capitalism. I do not believe that this is an appropriate way of posing the problem apparently involved here.

I think that having an awareness for that dimension in Marx's thought that is informed by what he calls the "artistic approach" may hopefully lead to a new reading of "*Das Kapital*", a reading that, in other words, knows of the circumstance that Marx himself had aimed at overcoming his own "theoretical" way of understanding. I think that Marx did believe that the theoretical approach can overcome the dangers that are inbuilt into it, namely those of the idealist or conceptual onesidedness, if the theoretical approach remains grounded in the materially-concrete *in a bodily way*. Doing this is, of course, a difficult task in the analysis of capital. But Marx also knows that there are more adequate ways of understanding than even the theoretical-critical one, since these other ways, besides the artistic, the practical-mental and religious ones, are better protected against sheerly mental acrobatics and the "dialectic balancing of concepts" a la Hegel. Marx had reached a level from where we too could regain that "rare condition" under which a way of understanding is not only capable of its simultaneous critique, like in a "practical-mental" approach, but is even carried by a new naivete gained after having gone through the pains of Capitalism. Our question now is: Do we, in a bodily grounded way, share the range in the modes of understanding that Marx is aware of, as it reaches from a theoretical approach (in the materialist sense) to a practical-mental one and finally to an artistic sense for the world? If we do, then we will be able to accept Marx's still cold blooded analysis of Capitalism and synthesize it, as he did, with our warm blooded affirmation of man's communist essence.

Bibliography

Adler, Max: *Das Soziologische in Kants Erkenntniskritik*, Vienna (*Verlag der Wiener Volksbuchhandlung*) 1924.

Barion, Jakob: *Hegel und die marxistische Staatslehre*, Bonn (*Bouvier Verlag*) 1970.

Bloch, Ernst: *Das Prinzip Hoffnung*, Frankfurt (*Suhrkamp Verlag*) 1959.

Habermas, Jürgen: *Erkenntnis und Interesse*, Frankfurt (*Suhrkamp Verlag*) 1968.

Hegel, Georg Wilhelm Friedrich: *Phänomenologie des Geistes*, Frankfurt (*Suhrkamp Verlag*) 1970 (vol. III of G.W.F. Hegel: *Werke in 20 Bänden)*.

Hegel, Georg Wilhelm Friedrich: *Grundlinien der Philosophie des Rechts*, Frankfurt (*Suhrkamp Verlag*) 1970 (vol. VII of G.W.F. Hegel: *Werke in 20 Bänden*).

Lieber, Hans-Joachim & Kautsky, Benedikt (eds.): *Karl - Marx - Ausgabe*, vols. 1 - 6, Darmstadt (*Wissenschaftliche Buchgesellschaft*) 1971.

Martin, Gottfried: *Immanual Kant - Ontologie und Wissenschaftstheorie*, Cologne (*Kölner Universitätsverlag*) 1958.

Marx, Karl: "*Grundrisse*", Moscow (Foreign Language Publishers) 1939 (vol. 1), 1941 (vol. 2).

Marx, Karl: "*Grundrisse*", (East-) Berlin (*Dietz Verlag*) 1953, 1974 (2nd edition).

Marx, Karl: "*Grundrisse*", Frankfurt (Europäische Verlagsanstalt), Vienna (*Europa Verlag*) n.d.

Marx, Karl: "*Grundrisse*", translated into English by Martin Nicolaus, New York (Penguin Books) 1973.

Marx, Karl & Engels, Friedrich: *Historisch-kritische Gesamtausgabe* (widely known as MEGA), ed. by D. Rjazanov & V. Adoratskij), Frankfurt, Berlin 1927 - 1932.

Marx, Karl & Engels, Friedrich: *Werke* (widely known as MEW), vols. I - XXXIX, (East-) Berlin (*Dietz Verlag*) 1956ff.

Reich, Klaus: *Die Vollständigkeit der kantischen Urteilstafel*, Berlin 1932.

Schiller, Friedrich V.: *Sämtliche Werke*, 16 vols. ed. by Eduard von der Hellen, Stuttgart (Cotta) 1904 - 1905.

Schmied-Kowarzik, Wolfdietrich: *Das dialektische Verhältnis des Menschen zur Natur*, Freiburg, Munich (Verlag Karl Alber) 1984.

Schmidt, Alfred: *Der Begriff der Natur in der Lehre von Marx*, Frankfurt (*Europäische Verlagsanstalt*) 1962.